NATIVE HEADMAN, CENTRAL LIBERIA.

THE
BLACK REPUBLIC

LIBERIA; ITS POLITICAL AND SOCIAL CONDITIONS TO-DAY

BY

HENRY FENWICK REEVE, C.M.G.
(Late Colonial Secretary Gambia)

WITH AN INTRODUCTION BY
SIR ALFRED SHARPE, K.C.M.G., C.B.

NEGRO UNIVERSITIES PRESS
NEW YORK

24-2342

Originally published in 1923
by H. F. & G. Witherby, London

Reprinted 1969 by
Negro Universities Press
A DIVISION OF GREENWOOD PUBLISHING CORP.
NEW YORK

SBN 8371-1412-8

PRINTED IN UNITED STATES OF AMERICA

"Love of Liberty brought us here."
(Motto of the Liberian Republic.)

PREFACE

For several years past the author of these notes has been convinced that it is the conscientious duty of every sincere friend of the African races to bring under the notice of the Powers which have recognized the independence of the Liberian Republic the failure of the rulers of that State to make good their promises, and to keep in line with the great civilizing efforts of other Governments on the west coast of Africa.

Twenty years of experience, and the knowledge gained of the splendid progress made by European Powers in their endeavours to bring the Tropical Belt across the Continent more and more into line with the enlightenment and civilization of the twentieth century, entitles one who has been a pioneer and humble worker in that vast field of practical work of the Christian nations, to ask the rulers of the Liberian Republic, " What hast thou done with thy talent?" How hast thou repaid the parental kindness, both sentimental and practical, that the great Powers, England, France, and America, have consistently evinced towards thy little State, for the best part of a century?

The answer is contained in the statements made herein, written after several visits and a residence in the Interior for part of three successive dry seasons.

In revealing the actual internal conditions of the State, the author has been careful to speak of things as they are, "To nothing extenuate, nor set down aught in malice." The statements made are not the result of hasty judgments of passing events, but may be regarded as well-drawn conclusions after several visits, fortified by inquiries from all classes of the Liberian community; and, although in some directions the information is not drawn from personal experience, it can be confirmed by reputable witnesses.

In order that they may also be supported by written testimony, the author proposes to draw largely upon the most recent works on the general state of the Republic and its Government, and therefore cites at length statements made by Professor Frederick Starr, in his able and comprehensive con-

PREFACE

tribution to the available literature on the subject, written in 1911-12 ("Liberia," by Frederick Starr, Chicago, 1913).

Professor Starr, in his turn, has quoted liberally from former authorities, notably Mr. G. W. Ellis, for some years secretary to the United States Legation at Monrovia, and M. Delafosse, sometime Consul for France to Liberia, whose observations cover approximately the period 1900 to 1910. All three of these authorities are actuated by friendly feelings toward the Liberians and show that friendliness in their writings; but, as will be seen, all three regard themselves in a position to speak the truth with regard to the internal conditions and shortcomings of the Government of the Republic.

The masterly work of Sir Harry Johnston, "Liberia" (London, 1906), has also been drawn upon for confirmation of statements made by the other authors, and where applicable the references are quoted. Professor Starr does not agree with Sir Harry Johnston's statistics with regard to the population of Liberia, but as the latter is so well known as a careful and experienced observer his figures have been adopted.

Sir Harry Johnston is also a friend of Liberia and

the Liberians, and his splendid book testifies to his kindly interest in the little Black Republic.

The author has been a consistent friend of native races and a supporter of their interests during forty years spent working amongst them; and it is purely on these grounds, and on behalf of the indigenous tribes of Liberia, that he now poses as a candid critic, and in the words of the celebrated apostle of Right and Justice boldly says to the rulers thereof, " J'accuse."

H. F. R.

INTRODUCTION

This book was one of a number of manuscripts by Henry Fenwick Reeve. It was intended for publication in 1921, but his death prevented this. His friends, knowing the love he had for Africa and the Africans, and the depth of his feeling regarding Liberia, felt it would be wrong that his views, as expressed in these pages, should not be placed before the public.

Henry Reeve was a many-sided man. Alike as administrator, architect, civil engineer, geologist and surveyor he made his mark. He was a copious but singularly exact writer, chiefly on African subjects. He was of old English stock in the County of Kent, where he was born in 1854. He went, while a boy, to Australia, where he passed into the Public Service after several years spent at the Melbourne University.

Soon after reaching twenty he began a career as a Civil Servant, which was to continue for something like forty years. Engineering and public works in general were his special professional province, and he carried out work in this sphere for several governments. For a while he kept to Australia, holding posts under the Governments of New South Wales and Victoria, but soon decided to range farther afield, and thus began his connection with the Tropical Dependencies, which was to last for the rest of his official life, except for a period during which he served in Newfoundland. There, as also in Lagos, and in Fiji, he worked with Sir William MacGregor, with whom he formed one of the most valued friendships of his life.

Mr. Roeve's work in West Africa had been preceded by a term of stiff work in Fiji, the chief town of which, Suva, was laid out by him. On the west coast of Africa he was occupied partly in the old Lagos Colony, of which he was for a period Acting Governor, and partly in Gambia, where he ended as Colonial Secretary. During his term of office he acted as Chief Commissioner of the Anglo-French Boundary Commission, which was at work in 1895-6 and again in 1898-9; and soon after the conclusion of his services on the latter occasion he received the C.M.G.

INTRODUCTION

As a Civil Servant Mr. Reeve is still, in both the West African Dependencies just named, remembered with the affectionate respect which people rarely fail to extend to those who are able, honest and generous. But his interest in West Africa was far from ceasing with his official connection. He wrote and published, a few years ago, a book on the Gambia, which is still, and will probably long remain, the classical work. While he had a warm regard for our Allies of France, he was an active, indefatigable British patriot, and both in public and in private represented strongly the injustice and impolicy of leaving a country with the loyal people and wonderful resources of the Gambia in uncertainty as to whether it was to be British or French. He never tired of telling those interested of the immense potentialities of West Africa. He practised what he preached, for he spent thousands of pounds of his private funds upon experiments in the Gambia, and also interested himself greatly in the development of Liberia.

Reeve went to Liberia on behalf of the Liberian Development Company to investigate and report on their gold and diamond propositions in the Republic. His work resulted in the finding of extensive gold deposits, and in the initiation of dredging operations. He also found diamonds, and was convinced that both these propositions could be worked profitably. The European War, however, and shortness of capital, put an end, for the time being at any rate, to active work. It was during the periods he thus spent in Liberia that he put together the notes for this book.

Henry Reeve was an earnest advocate for safeguarding the rights of the aboriginal tribes in Africa. No one understood natives better or was more in sympathetic touch with them. The conditions prevailing in the Republic of Liberia impressed him very strongly. While in sympathy with the ideals of the original founders of the Liberian Settlement, he arrived at the distinct opinion that the attempt to establish a Black Republic in West Africa on civilized lines had ended in utter failure, and that the worst point in it was the handing over of some two millions of aboriginal tribes to the tender mercies of a band of a few thousand American negroes.

My own experience of Liberia consists of two visits made during 1919-20-21, during which I

INTRODUCTION

spent six months in the country. On the first occasion I entered the Republic by way of the Sierra Leone Railway from Freetown to Pendembu, as this enabled me to get at once to the Liberian Hinterland and to dispense with the troubles and difficulties experienced in getting up country from Monrovia, as there are practically no means of transport in the Republic and no roads. On the journey I traversed all the Hinterland of the western half of Liberia, and eventually reached the coast at Monrovia, following down the valleys of the Lofa and St. Paul Rivers. On my second visit I landed at Monrovia and went up country to the Boporo district, also visiting some of the coast settlements.

I always met with kindness and friendliness on the part of the Liberian Government and officials, and believe that under President King they are doing their best—in their own way—to establish a reasonable administration of the country. But there can be no question that—as Mr. Reeve states—this experiment of the establishment of a Black Republic in West Africa, to amalgamate the aboriginal inhabitants, and to teach them to govern themselves, has been an entire failure. The most striking feature of this failure is that a few thousand coast negroes, by means of an armed force, equipped with modern rifles, field guns, etc., and officered by American negroes, are able to more or less keep in subjection, to tax, to levy from, and in many ways to treat as inferior races, some two million industrious, capable, and naturally well disposed aboriginal inhabitants.

Soldiers of the " Liberian Frontier Force " take what they want from natives in villages in the Interior. If there is opposition then comes trouble. Anyone who has had to do with Africa knows what native soldiers are when the strictest control is not exercised over them, and when they are given power of any kind: they become a pest; and in Liberia are a common cause of the misunderstandings and wars which arise from time to time.

There is no more valuable asset to any country than its native population. In Liberia large districts have been practically depopulated owing to wars with the aboriginal tribes.

The payment of a hut tax in civilized African territories is supposed to be a contribution by the aboriginal inhabitants to a Government which secures for them peace, a good and just administra-

INTRODUCTION 19

tion, easy means of communication, opportunities for trade, educational facilities, medical treatment, and, generally, the benefits of civilization. The Liberian Government draws a considerable revenue from the Hinterland people, but gives them little or nothing in return. Beyond the coast belt there are no roads, no good footpaths, no permanent bridges, no telegraphs, no postal system, no adequate magisterial provision, no agricultural effort, no medical or educational facilities, no public works. The Interior exists for two Government purposes—the extraction of as much revenue as possible—and the provision of a number of billets for coast men.

I was much impressed by the inland tribes of Liberia. They are among the finest and most capable Africans I have met in Tropical Africa, and only require good government, sympathetic treatment, and development of the country by railways and roads to become great producers. There is no sympathy whatever between them and the coast Government: it is only the arms and ammunition at the disposal of the latter which enable them to exist.

The Americo-Liberian is not industrious. Monrovia, the capital, lives largely on tinned goods, has scarcely any supply of vegetables or fruit, and imports hundreds of tons of rice for local consumption. In this district where the Americo-Liberians have many small settlements, a moderate display of energy and industry could raise a sufficient amount of fruit, vegetables, rice, poultry, and farm produce to keep Monrovia going and to supply shipping.

The capital town of Liberia is prettily situated on hilly ground, and the appearance of the place from the sea is pleasing and picturesque. The inner harbour is the estuary of the Mesurado Creek, into which run several other creeks, the Stockton communicating with the St. Paul River, the Wotherspoon Creek, and others. Monrovia has thus a fair amount of inland water communications, which might at moderate expense be improved. The streets, though wide, are impassable except for foot traffic, as they are a mass of rocks.

In Monrovia there are few people who have been thirty miles inland. This applies not only to Liberians but to Europeans, and is partly accounted for by the fact that under existing Liberian laws no one may go inland without a permit. Moreover,

INTRODUCTION

no European trader is allowed to establish trading stations up-country.

Liberia is a rich country, and is at present the one totally undeveloped stretch of West Africa. As there is no means of transport inland—none of its rivers being navigable for more than a few miles —there is under existing conditions no possibility of development, even if its Government encouraged the trading community to exploit the Interior, which is not the case. Comparing the central and most inland districts of Liberia with similar districts in Sierra Leone, there can be no doubt that the former are much richer in oil palms. Liberia also has great mineral possibilities. Wherever, in West Africa, the oil palm grows in fair quantities, and there is a native population, it will pay on that account alone, to construct railways. Railways are the only means by which Tropical Africa can be developed. Roads serve up to certain limits: but the bed-rock test is the cost per ton mile, and this for motor traffic in West Africa is certainly not less than one shilling and sixpence (often more), whereas rail transport should be done for twopence.

So far as climate goes Liberia may be divided into three zones:

(a) The Upper Hinterland, where the general elevation is on an average about 1,500 feet above sea level.

(b) The Central Zone, round about 500 to 700 feet.

(c) The Coastal Zone, from 400 feet downwards.

In the Upper Hinterland the climate in the dry season is pleasant.

In the Central Zone you get pleasant mornings, but the middle hours and afternoons become unbearably hot, with oppressive nights.

The Coastal Zone has much the same climate as the Central, but is damper (not the same dry heat).

In all the inland districts cotton is grown by the natives, and spun into thread, from which "country cloths" are woven on roughly constructed looms. Every village has its weavers. Some of their cloth is dyed blue (with home-grown indigo), and the favourite pattern is alternate stripes of blue and white.

In the Hinterland Mandingo traders from French territory bring horses, cattle, calabashes, and various articles of trade, buying in return chiefly kola nuts and rice, both of which are largely produced in districts near the inland frontier.

INTRODUCTION

One travels in Liberia, not only in the Hinterland districts, but right down to the coast belt, on native paths, always in forest, as practically the whole of the Republic is covered with dense forest. What one longs for is some open country and a view, which is never to be had. The paths run up and down steep hills, are a few inches wide, and are crossed in every direction by creepers and tree roots of all sizes. Stumps and rocks are also everywhere. Many tree trunks lie—where they fall—across the paths, and have to be climbed over.

Liberia is remarkably free from noxious beasts: no lions, leopards which seem seldom to attack human beings unless molested, few crocodiles in the Interior, few snakes, not many districts where tsetse fly are troublesome, and I saw no housticks and few jiggers: many districts are more or less free from mosquitoes.

Looking to the future I can see little hope of progress in Liberia under the present system of government of a large slice of West Africa, holding some two million aboriginal natives, by a few thousand alien negroes from America and elsewhere. They have had their chance, and have shown themselves to be incapable of civilized government.

There will be little hope of proper treatment of the inland tribes, of just treatment of the population, of honest government, or of any advance in civilization, and development of the country's resources, till every branch of administration is taken over and supervised by some civilized power or powers. The "ruling caste" has shown itself to be incapable. The conduct of affairs in Monrovia, and the other coast settlements, has been poor enough, but succeeding Governments' dealings with the Interior tribes have been reprehensible. These inland natives are naturally peaceful and industrious: they put up with bad treatment till it reaches breaking point; then they either clear over the borders and become settlers in a new land (Sierra Leone or French territory), or they put up active opposition, which means military action against them. Liberia is being slowly but steadily ruined. These native "wars" are not conducted on the same lines as those on which the British have carried out such military expeditions as have been necessary in West Africa. In Liberia the military force is accompanied by a large contingent of native "allies," whose operations chiefly consist in finishing off the work carried out by the military, looting, and seizing all the people they can, who are afterwards disposed of either by retaining as serfs or selling over the borders to other tribes. It must be realized that African tribes are seldom united, and that one tribe is always glad of the opportunity of raiding another.

The purchase of young people is quite common in Liberia: it is called "pawning." The price ranges from about three pounds to four pounds. The person pawned becomes the property of the purchaser, but is supposed to be redeemable by payment of the price originally paid. Children thus obtained by Liberians are almost invariably well treated; many of them are given some education. Probably their lives are just as happy as they would have been in their own environs. I was told that it is seldom any of them attempt to run away.

On what precise lines some reorganization of the Government of Liberia should be undertaken by the Powers is not for me to say. International control has never been a great success in any part of the world, but anything is better than the present state of affairs.

However desirous the leaders of the Americo-

INTRODUCTION

Liberians may be to improve their administration, they have no capable, honest body of their class on which to draw for officials. If every corrupt official of the administration were dismissed to-morrow there is no better material with which to replace them.

Perhaps the worst example of Americo-Liberian Government is the Inland District Administration. There are few—if any—honest District Commissioners, and many are hopelessly corrupt and unscrupulous: yet these are the men on whom depend good or bad relations with the aboriginal tribes, and whose action may cause uprisings and wars.

Some time ago it seemed likely that the United States Government were going to make a loan of five million dollars to Liberia. The conditions for the granting of this loan were somewhat onerous, and possibly were felt by the Liberians as humiliating, as they placed almost every department of the Republic under the control of officials to be appointed by America. The conditions were, however, accepted by Liberia, as the Government stands in pressing and immediate need of funds in order to pay their current expenses and salaries.

INTRODUCTION

They are already largely indebted. The United States, however, finally vetoed the loan, and it is difficult to understand how the Liberian Government is able at the present date to carry on.

Liberia has very great possibilities. It is a rich country, but no development is possible under existing conditions. The country is a blot on West Africa. It has all the essentials for prosperity, a very fine inland population, rich land, existing products for export. It only requires two essentials: good government and means of transport.

Little is ever heard of the country. Henry Reeve's book may serve to make the existing conditions better known.

A. S.

CONTENTS

CHAP.		PAGE
	PREFACE	9
	INTRODUCTION	13
I.	GENERAL CONDITIONS	33
II.	INTERNAL CONDITIONS	43
III.	ADMINISTRATION OF JUSTICE	81
IV.	THE LIBERTY OF THE SUBJECT	109
V.	EDUCATION	143
VI.	SANITATION	153
VII.	COMMUNICATIONS	161
VIII.	EXTERNAL RELATIONS	169
IX.	DEVIL WORSHIP	183
X.	THE SUMMING UP	195
	INDEX	205

LIST OF ILLUSTRATIONS

NATIVE HEADMAN, CENTRAL LIBERIA	*Frontispiece*	
HOUSES IN MONROVIA	*Facing page*	40
A LOCAL "QUEEN," ST. PAUL RIVER	,,	50
A "CIVILIZED" LIBERIAN	,,	62
A PALAVER WITH CHIEFS, UPPER LIBERIA	,,	94
VILLAGE AND NATIVES, LIBERIAN INTERIOR	,,	112
A "KING'S" DAUGHTER, MIDDLE ST. PAUL VALLEY	,,	134
A LIBERIAN "ROAD" NEAR THE COAST	,,	164
MUD WALLS ROUND VILLAGE, FRANCO-LIBERIAN BORDER	,,	190

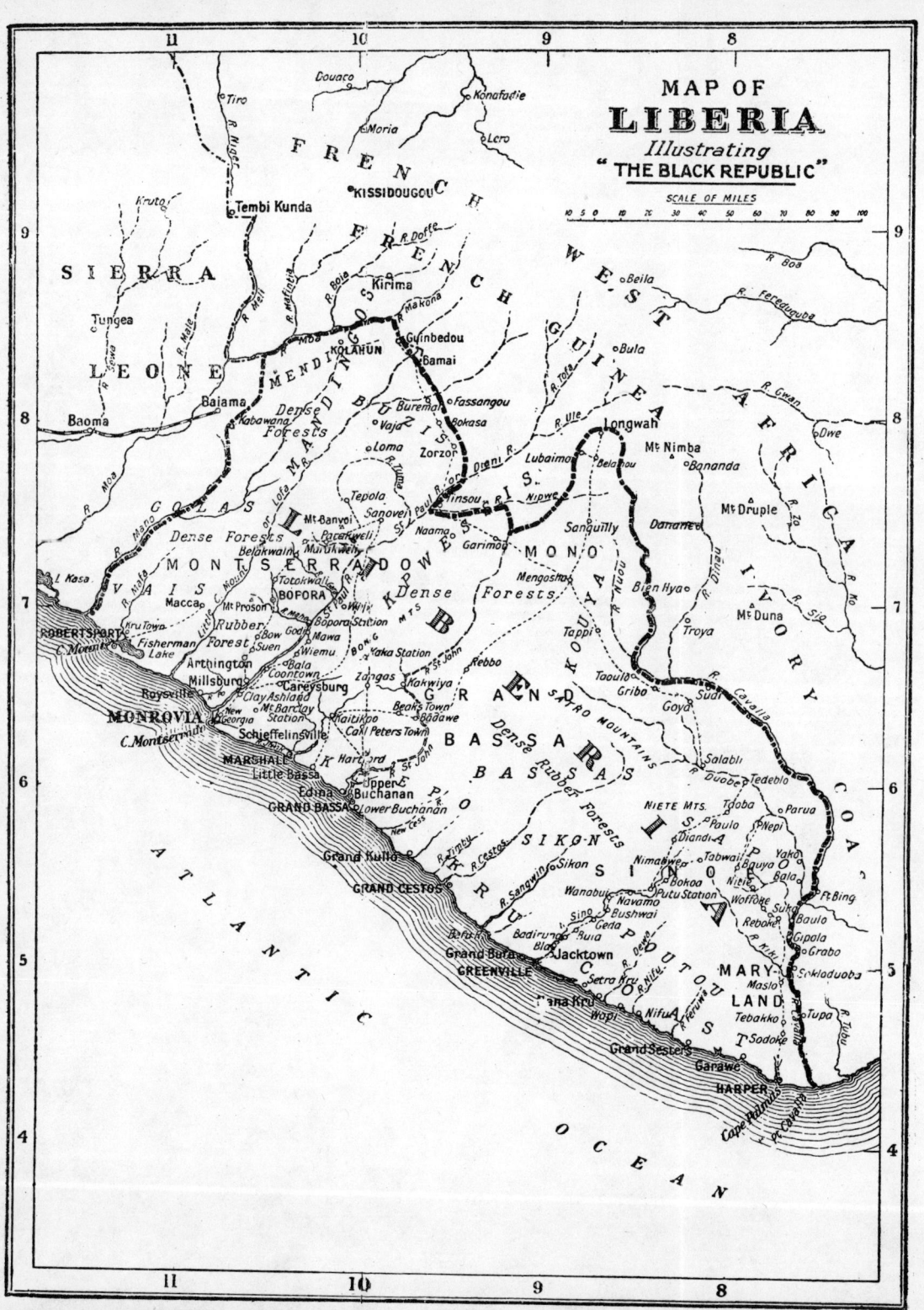

CHAPTER I

GENERAL CONDITIONS

GENERALLY speaking the Constitution laid down, under which the Republic is supposed to be governed, is an excellent form of government from a theoretic point of view, but from ignorance and laxity in the administration of its principles the whole régime has lapsed into corruption of late years, both at Headquarters and in the Provinces. The Constitution was based upon that of the United States, and the first set of statutes was drawn up by Greenleaf, the well-known American author of several standard American Law Books.

He was charged with this work by the American Colonization Society, and his scheme was accepted *in toto* for the new State.

The Liberian Constitution, therefore, with its

organic statutory laws, was not evolved out of the natural conditions and surroundings of Liberian life, but was super-imposed from without.

As Liberians were without the education of the schools from which the laws were evolved it was natural for them to stumble and fall in the attempt to administer and carry into effect a system of law-giving handed to them complete and up-to-date from the United States, which was based upon conditions resulting from centuries of civilization, although originally derived from precedents that had ceased to exist with the older State. while they were now commencing with the newly born State of Liberia. The working of such a Constitution was, therefore, extremely difficult, even to honest rulers striving to apply such laws; and after many additions to meet the actual conditions of life, the acts of successive Legislatures gradually took the place of the ideal Constitution; so that practically all the power became vested in the President of the day, who, with the support that the "Ins" invariably get against the "Outs," could pass what legislation he desired; and he is to-day an autocrat instead of merely the chief citizen trusted as the upholder of the Constitution.

GENERAL CONDITIONS

Having arrived at that stage, it is only human nature that the autocrat should fortify his position, which leads to dispensing favours to his supporters; and appointments are now practically farmed out to the supporters of the President, or other State Officials of his Party, with but little consideration for the honesty or ability of the chosen ones, provided they are sound supporters of the Party through thick and thin. It naturally follows that the more supporters the stronger the position of the Chief, and this again leads to the multiplication of offices both in Monrovia (the capital) and throughout the Provinces. The payment of this army of hungry politicians depletes the funds of the Republic, and results in the suspension or stoppage of useful public works for want of funds.

Moreover, as the Treasury is generally empty, even where a sufficient salary is allotted to the office in question, the official often remains unpaid, either in part or altogether, and is allowed to pay himself out of fees and other forms of revenue passing through his hands; or, when these have to be strictly accounted for (as with the Customs Department which is under the control of Foreign Receivers for the repayment of the Consolidated

Loan), Liberian Officials resort to supplementary charges practically unauthorized, or levied in some form or other; and these are paid by the public, because appeal to higher authority has been found to be a loss of both time and money, especially when the appeal takes a legal form. The underpaid condition of the Government staff also leads to improper collusion between that body and the public, and results in injustice to the individual, or the subversion of the principle of the administration of impartial justice.

The important official, with a wife and family and appearances to keep up, has to resort at times to a loan, and as his fellow officials, from whom it might be more regular to borrow a little money, are in the same state, it follows that his needs are supplied by members of the community he helps to govern, generally by foreigners, and possibly from those whom he is in a position to benefit in the administration of his official duties, and so on to the irregular position of being under deep obligations to an individual against whom it may be his duty to give an adverse decision.

Sir Harry Johnston deals with this point as follows: "We are given to boasting in our own

GENERAL CONDITIONS 37

country of the pure tone of our official life and its relative freedom from corruption, in plain words, the more or less unbribable nature of our officials."

" This happy state of affairs is brought about not by any deeper attachment on the part of the Briton to abstract morality, but because, for a long time past, we have realized that to secure impartial and incorruptible officials we must pay men sufficiently well to place them above temptation. This principle is not yet realized in some parts of Europe and America, and certainly not in Liberia. In these regions it is very often impossible for a subordinate official to live within his means, on his official income; consequently in some cases, severe temptations are put in his way to add to that income by illicit means. There are, of course, officials, high and low, in Liberia of absolute integrity and as high-souled in their ideas as the men we have in our own service. But, again, there have been in the past others—as there would be in England under similar circumstances—not above taking a monetary inducement to depart from their strict duty. This has been hitherto one of the weaknesses of the custom service in Liberia. High-handed officers of European steamers or influential merchants have used both threats and monetary blandishments to evade the strict payment of duties, export and import."

The German Colony was the centre of this cancerous evil, which has gradually destroyed the independence of the official class, and the traders of that nation were known to be the creditors of influential members of the Legislature, high officials, and even of the rank and file. Hence the overpowering influence of the Germans before the war in Liberian affairs.

As to the handling of public moneys—although actual theft is not suggested, and moreover, if detected is punished more or less severely according to the position of the official involved and his social position or influence upon the powers that be—malversation of funds is a common practice, and few, if any, of the higher officials distinguish between " Meum and Teum," in that sense. A high official uses whatever funds come through his hands for his own purposes and distributes to his retainers down the line at his own sweet will, so that all are in the swim, and no man therefore can lay a charge against another. There is, however, a penalty, in the loss of office, for what is known by the euphemism " Eating too hoggishly."

GENERAL CONDITIONS

Before the establishment of the first American Receivers a large sum was annually left in the Treasury unappropriated. That sum was playfully called "Hog," and whenever money was required for any purpose, either public or private, for which there was no specific appropriation, the decision was invariably "We'll go to Hog."

The above conditions weigh heavily upon the non-official or tax-paying classes, leading also to high import duties and other forms of taxation, mostly used to pay the officials; for little is expended on the towns in the way of streets, roads, and other communications, and nothing at all in the Interior. There are practically no sanitary authorities or efficient sanitary works, excepting spasmodic attempts to clean up the streets at intervals by prison labour. The sea front, and the landing places or wharves of Monrovia, the capital and chief commercial city of the Republic, are a disgrace.

Here, if anywhere, heavy taxation should show some return in the form of facilities for dealing with passengers and goods, as in other ports on the west coast; but the comparison epitomizes the hopeless condition of the whole territory. The fore-shore reeks with the filth of years, the wharves are out of repair, and little attempt has been made to reclaim or straighten the sea front, on which jetties and stores are scattered higgledy-piggledy. The street along the shore follows the same pattern of lack of arrangement; no attempt has been made to improve upon the natural conditions, or to align the buildings on some considered plan for future improvement of the port and surroundings, or to reclaim the low ground which has received the filth and ordure of the upper parts of the town for many years.

With regard to the main street of the town of Monrovia a certain amount of credit should be given for the progress made in building. Twenty years ago there were few substantial houses excepting those built by foreign merchants as residences on the hill overlooking the harbour.

These, with the small native houses connecting them in the main street, gave the impression of a mouth with several fine teeth left in place and a row of blackened stumps between. The gaps have been more or less filled up now, and other residents have joined up with stone houses; but little has been done in the way of street formation, footpaths, or channels, which the rating of these fine houses would suggest; so the general public stumbles over

HOUSES IN MONROVIA, THE LIBERIAN CAPITAL.

rocks and hillocks and cannot travel safely in the town after dark without the personal lantern of the Dark Ages.

The alignment of the main streets (although some lead precipitately to the beach) and the stone houses suggest prosperity and progress; while a French and a German wireless station, the latter on the slope of Signal Hill and commanding the town, give quite an up-to-date appearance from the sea. One remarks these features in passing, and might conclude that all was well with the little State.

This general air of well-doing is also emphasized by the Liberian and Mission Colleges, and the churches and mission stations which show up boldly on the coast or on the rivers; but a few months spent among the native races in the Interior will disclose a state of being very little removed from the primitive condition in which they existed before the white man came to West Africa, unless one accepts taxation, both direct and indirect, as a sign of progress—though for this the indigenous tribes get very little, if any, return.

But the Liberian Government, in common with other Governments of West African Colonies, is in the position of trustee and guardian of the indigenous races to whom the country actually belongs, and it is in this capacity that their progress is to be judged, not by the civilized appearance of the town of Monrovia, or the small areas of settled and cultivated land surrounding their settlements on the coast.

One may go a step further and point out that it is the more incumbent on the Liberio-Americans to fulfil faithfully their trusteeship, inasmuch as they have specially charged themselves with the welfare of their fellow Africans; and it is this trust which forms their only claim to territory and to sovereignty over the people of the country. It is only the long deferred hope from the date of the foundation of their state, of the due performance of this self-imposed duty, that has entitled them to the recognition of other colonizing powers, and justifies their existence as a State on the Continent of Africa.

CHAPTER II

INTERNAL CONDITIONS

Part I—Explanatory

PEOPLE one converses with at home on the subject of Liberia are under the impression—amounting in some cases to conviction—that the Republic was founded by Philanthropic American and other societies, as a genuine effort to found a State where all Africans, whether from America or indigenous peoples of Africa, should both learn and enjoy for all time the benefits of Freedom; and this actually was the ideal of the founders.

The American people regarded the experiment with a favourable eye as a possible solution of their great colour question, and, therefore, extended a non-committal and rather indolent form of encouragement to what might be regarded as not quite a legitimate daughter. Owing to the converse application of their Monro Doctrine, effective action towards an actual Protectorate which would introduce new factors into the already intricate problem of the "Scramble for Africa" by the European Powers, did not receive encouragement from any of the Chancelleries of those Powers interested.

The impression prevails that the American Pioneers in Liberia were welcomed with open arms by their fellow Africans as saviours of their independence and freedom.

That is the view constantly put forth by the Liberio-Americans, and grandiloquent speeches both at home and abroad, with the rhodomontades of the Liberian Press on the text of the motto of the Republic and of the Liberian Order of Redemption "The Love of Liberty brought us here," have served for years to throw dust in the eyes of the world; while the present writer, when first visiting Monrovia, also had the impression of a benevolent, though rather indolent, form of Government that had attracted the surrounding tribes to throw in their lot with their fellow negroes from America in preference to being under the protection of one or other of the European Powers.

The author's first awakening came through reading a history of the country from the landing of the first mission in 1822, written by an American visitor[1] who adopted the useful but always thankless attitude of the candid friend, and showed plainly that even Perseverance Island, the first landing-place on the beach at the mouth of the Mesurado River, and afterwards the promontory of Mesurado, had to be defended by force of arms against the coast tribes whom the Missionaries came to redeem from savagery. From those early days until the widely extended territory closed with Sierra Leone on the west and with the French Ivory Coast on the east, the history is a succession of wars, and simply repeats the history of other Powers in their conflicts with native tribes in Africa.

A permission to live on the coast from the Chief, a plot on which to build the store house or settlement, further territory acquired by Treaty in return for a few trumpery presents, interference with native rights and customs, consequent retaliation by the stoppage of trade roads, the fight, large or small, where the primitive arrow and spear were opposed to modern rifles, the natives trying to drive the intruders from their territories back into the sea,

[1] " Liberia." Description, History, Problems, by Frederick Starr, Chicago, 1913.

sometimes successfully for a time; but the end always the same—more rifles and guns come over the sea and the Chief's town is burnt. Victory is followed by an assertion of sovereignty over the lands overrun, by a new title of " Conquest by War," and, as the doctors say, " The mixture to be repeated," up the coast, down the coast, and as far into the Interior as it was safe to penetrate for the time. This mixture is known to diplomacy as " Peaceful Penetration," a euphemism which in practice means that the penetrated have to take everything lying down, while the penetration is carried out as described above.

From an ethical point of view, acquisition in Africa of the lands of the Africans is based upon similar false titles, and in this direction the Liberian, excepting for the fact that he has not improved the conditions of the native races, or brought any benefits in the train of Conquest, is no worse than his white neighbour; but what they both construed into a title to land by treaty is merely a right to occupy during the pleasure of the Chief and his people.

The Chief and the tribe may decide that there is no danger in allowing A or B to occupy a portion of the tribal lands for purposes of trade or cultivation, but native custom and tradition make it only a lease to be held during the pleasure of the lessors. During many years' experience in dealing with these matters the writer has found it to be almost the invariable rule that neither the tribe nor their Chiefs for the time being have the inclination or the power to divest themselves of the fee simple, any more than the holder of a life tenancy in entail can sell the property outright.

But although the white man might deal with natives in this high-handed manner the Liberian Mission and its descendants had come back to the land of their origin to free their kindred from such oppression, and in their own words: " To form a Free Republic as a nucleus around which other African states, having freed themselves from their oppressors (presumably by force) should nucleate, until the whole Continent rings with the cry of Freedom of a special brand." Their title to wield a Sovereign Power over what is now called Liberia has never been acknowledged by most of the tribes; while fighting against the " Americans " is the daily occupation of some of them.

Part II—Historical

The following synopsis is taken from Professor Starr's book, and the whole work is well worth careful reading and study.

The Pioneers reached Mesurado in December, 1882, and having examined the surroundings commenced negotiations with the paramount Chief of the district, King Peter, and, on payment of one-half the agreed price in trade, eventually secured a contract from him, and five other kings, for a stretch of coast, including the Cape and mouth of the Mesurado River, with undefined boundaries inland.

The first settlement was on Perseverance Island and as more and more Colonists were added to the settlement the natives became suspicious of the peaceful character of their mission. They were informed that King Peter had no right to sell the lands of the people, and they were requested to take back the amount of trade given, and to leave at once.

INTERNAL CONDITIONS

Before this "palaver" was settled another arose about the possession of a vessel which had drifted ashore with slaves on board.

She was prize to a British sloop of war, and had the prize crew on board. When the King sent his people to take possession in accordance with the custom of rights to flotsam and jetsam they were met with resistance and beaten off for the time. The captain of the vessel, knowing that the next attack would be more formidable, asked the Agent of the Colonists for help, which was given, together with a field gun, so that the natives were again beaten back with considerable loss; but the stranded vessel went to pieces, and most of the stores were lost. When the natives attacked again the crew were exposed on the beach and were killed, together with one Colonist.

The natives had only been paid one part of the purchase goods, and they now returned it, refusing to receive the balance; and thus, according to their native customs, annulled the transaction. To this the Colonists would not agree, and the natives, having asked the Agent and others to a "palaver" in their town, seized them as hostages and held them until a promise was given to receive back the purchase money and to leave the coast. Having given the promise and obtained his release the Agent appears to have appealed to a more powerful Chief inland, who gave a decision upholding the original transaction. As a first attempt to civilize the races they had come to serve this primary transaction does not strike one as quite calculated to impress the tribes with that sense of justice and equity without which all efforts on the part of would-be civilizers are void and useless, and, moreover, the Colonists had now a blood feud with the people owing to their interference in a " palaver " that did not concern them.

When the Colony was moved to the promontory, they reaped the consequences of this breach of faith, and an actual state of war ensued between the Liberians and the natives, which became traditional and hereditary owing to the heavy loss of life due to the use of artillery against natives armed only with spears and bows and arrows. The Vendetta has been handed down from generation to generation, and as the territory was extended similar conditions arose.

Land taken by the sword must be held by the sword, and the present state of Liberia as

A LOCAL "QUEEN," ST. PAUL RIVER.

INTERNAL CONDITIONS 51

exemplified by the inaugural address of President Howard (quoted later on) is the natural sequence to the methods employed in establishing the State.

Fighting appears to have been as continuous in those early years as it is now, and it was only owing to occasional help from seaward that the Colonists were able to maintain their foothold on the promontory, having estranged all the surrounding tribes whose man power was unlimited when compared with their own forces.

And yet these were not blood-thirsty savages they were fighting against, but landowners who thought they had been unjustly deprived of their land. Land and the boundaries thereof are the most pregnant causes of warfare in Africa, or for that matter even in the civilized world; moreover, fighting was, and is still, the daily occupation of the tribes, so that the Colonists were never likely to obtain peace by force of arms; while had they been better acquainted with the psychology of the African, and, as followers of the Prince of Peace, had used diplomacy with material arguments in the shape of gifts, in all likelihood they would have been allowed to settle down in peace, always provided that they did not claim sovereignty over their land until they were strong enough to maintain it.

An instance of the kindly attitude of the natives towards the Colonists is given by Professor Starr who quotes from the annals of those days.

Seven children had been taken prisoners by the enemy, and two had been given up for a small gratuity, while five were retained and a larger ransom demanded, which it was decided not to pay.

" There was, however, a redeeming trait in their treatment of these helpless and tender captives. It was the first object of the captors to place them under the maternal care of several aged women, who, in Africa, as in most countries, are proverbially tender and indulgent. These protectresses had them clad in their usual habits, and at early periods of the truce sent to the Colony to inquire as to the proper kinds of food, and modes of preparing it, to which the youngest had been accustomed. The affections of their little charges were so perfectly won in the four months of their captivity as to oblige their own parents, at the end of that time, literally to tear away from their

INTERNAL CONDITIONS

keepers several of the youngest, amidst the most affectionate demonstrations of mutual attachment. Their gratuitous redemption was finally voted almost unanimously in a large council of native chiefs."

One would have thought that this amicable interlude would have led towards better relations between the Colonists and the native tribes, tending towards a scheme of occupation similar to that usually adopted by the British Government in their dealings with native landowners. There were not wanting examples of these methods in those days, as in the Gambia and Sierra Leone the necessary lands were leased from native Chiefs, while the Hinterland was a Protectorate ruled by the existing Chiefs, who were safeguarded against encroachment from without from intertribal wars as far as possible, and taught to rely upon the British Government for advice and protection during good behaviour.

In the Gambia, for example, the last of these original leases, that of the " Ceded Mile," was only included in the Colony by purchase in 1900 by the voluntary cession of the Kingdom of Barra, successive rulers of which had been maintained in authority and in their hereditary " Customs " of

"Three Bars"[1] for every ship that passed the "Pavilion" on Barra Point for about three hundred years (although in later years the ruling King was paid a yearly stipend in lieu thereof). It is almost unnecessary to add that there were hardly any troubles from native tribes when dealt with in this spirit of Right and Justice, and that our tenure has been peaceful on the whole, if one excepts the period when the French were invading the Hinterland of the Gambia, and the Boarder Chiefs made incursions into the territory. Or later on when an arbitrary international boundary was drawn in Paris which sliced the Hinterland into such pieces that no native could follow its ramifications, and which, moreover, practically cut across native States and all natural and intertribal boundaries, excepting the River Gambia itself.[2]

To return to Liberia, whose written history shows a continual ferment extending over the whole period of occupation up to the present date:

[1] A "bar" in olden times was a bar of iron about $6'' \times 2'' \times \frac{1}{4}''$, or its equivalent value in trade goods.

[2] The ancient kingdom of Barra lies on the north bank of the mouth of the River Gambia, opposite the island of St. Mary, on which Bathurst, the capital of the Colony, is situated. The pavilion of the King of Barra is a clump of high trees, which forms an excellent land-fall for vessels making the port.

INTERNAL CONDITIONS

A fair impression of the relations existing between Government and the tribes it is supposed to govern may be taken from the printed copies of President Howard's inaugural address in January, 1916, in which the following passage occurs.

Speaking of the services of the officers lent to the Republic by the United States, the President is reported to have said (quite in the style of the Powers recently fighting in Europe for their existence):

"All the officers so far procured have been under fire; the following wars have been fought: Tappi, August, 1912, to January, 1913, under Captain Browne; River Cess and Rock Cess, October, 1912, to April, 1913, under Major Ballard; Banei, July to November, 1913, under Captain Hawkins; Glassi, November, 1914, to February, 1915, under Lieutenants Martin and Miller; Pahn (Cape Palmas), April to June, 1915, under Captain Hawkins; Planh and Secomb, May, 1915"; and I may mention the war at Sinoe.

What manner of Government is this, which recounts civil strife as if it were an honourable adventure and a credit to themselves?

It may also be remembered that all these civil wars took place during President Howard's first term, and the irony of the fact is that he was elected for a second term, presumably to continue this warlike policy against the so-called subjects of the Liberian Government.

A month or two in the Interior with an observant eye for the outstanding features that ever mark the sphere of good government will convince anyone of the following fact:

That while the white man, and especially the "Ingliss," can travel through the country with perfect safety without an escort, on his acquired reputation for Justice and generosity, the Liberian must confine his travels to about twenty-five miles from the capital and to the coast elsewhere, unless he takes an escort for protection against the people he claims to be governing.

Part III—Social Relations

One of the reasons for the traditional hostility on the part of native races towards the Liberio-American lies in the fact that, although they are the original owners of the soil and lands of the territory, they have never been regarded as citizens of the Republic by its Liberio-American rulers, but rather as an inferior race of mankind; while their natural products, crops, and even their persons have always been looked upon as a field for exploitation in trading and taxation, and in the exportation of their young men to other Colonies as labourers.

In connection with this difference in status, Professor Starr writes under the head of " Economics ":

" We have already called attention to the attitude of the Americo-Liberian towards manual labour and have shown that it is, on the whole, natural under the circumstances. Where there are sharp contrasts between the elements of society, as there are in Liberia between the Americo-Liberians, the Vai, the Kroo, and the 'Bush Niggers,' there is bound to develop a more or less of caste feeling. This was inevitable with a people who had themselves come from a district where caste was as marked as in our southern states. The natives have never been considered the full equals of the emigrants, nor treated as brothers; they are 'hewers of wood' and 'drawers of water'; they are utilized as house servants. It is convenient to be able to fill one's house with 'Bush Niggers' as servants, and the settlers have done so from the early days of settlement."

"Why, indeed, should one himself work where life is easy, and money is quickly made through trade? This feeling of caste shows itself in various curious ways— thus the Colonists soon fell into the habit of calling themselves 'white men' in contrast to the negroes of the country."

Professor Starr here lays his finger on the centre of the trouble between the rulers and the ruled. To arrogate to oneself the position of the "white man" in Africa without the sense of right, justice, and the power to enforce one's decisions is a mere

INTERNAL CONDITIONS

travesty, and the natives of Liberia fully recognize this bombast on the part of the Americo-Liberians.

Native races are keenly alive to questions of social and racial precedence, and an attempt to gain prestige by a false assumption of racial superiority was bound to result in failure. Hence the natives of Liberia have never had the " Government they deserve."

In his preface Professor Starr also quotes at length from a former resident:

" One of the most thoughtful writers regarding the Republic is Delafosse, who, for a time, was French Consul at Monrovia. He has written upon Liberia on many occasions, and what he says always deserves consideration. On the whole he is not a hostile critic, having rather a friendly feeling towards Liberians, and being deeply interested in the Republic. We translate some passages from his writings, as his point of view is original. Delafosse says:

" ' If one considers the Liberians superficially—civilized, clad, knowing how to read and write, living in relatively comfortable houses—one will probably find them superior to the natives.

" ' Actually, they are rather inferior to them, as

well from the moral point of view, as from the point of view of general well-being.

"'First, along the coast and in the east, we see the Kroomen, a race of workers, energetic, proud, and fighters, but honest, rejoicing in a fine physical and moral health, jealous of the virtue of their women, of a most careful cleanliness.'

"What a contrast do they make by the side of the idle and nonchalant Liberians, expecting everything from the State, subject to every kind of congenital disease, and in particular to tuberculosis, never washing themselves, nourishing themselves with food that a native slave would not accept, decimated by a considerable mortality, having generally very few children, of whom, moreover, the greater part are born scrawny, weak, devoted beforehand to an early death!

"If we cast our eyes upon the natives of the west and north, the Vai and other tribes of the Mandingo, it is a different grade of comparison that offers itself to us, but always to the disadvantage of the Liberians. These natives half islamized, have, much more than the Liberians, the sentiment of human dignity, and their costume, fitted to the climate and the race, far from rendering them ridiculous, as the European (costume) does the Liberians, is not devoid of a certain æsthetic character. They have, the Vai and the Manienka, above all, a superior intelligence of commercial affairs. The Vai have even a self-civilization which makes this little tribe one of the most interesting peoples of Africa; alone, of all the negroes known, they possess a writing suited to the writing of their language, and this alphabet, which they have completely invented themselves, has no relationship with any other known alphabet.[1] A Vai native, named Momolu Massaquoi, established at Ghendimah, not far from the Anglo-Liberian boundary, a sort of model village, and in this village a school where he teaches the language and the literature of his country. I do not know what is the result of this attempt but it seems to me interesting, being an attempt purely indigenous in character towards perfectment, attempted alongside of the effort towards perfectionment by adaptation of European civilization which has so badly succeeded in Liberia."

Again, after having given an attractive description

[1] Sir Harry Johnston does not agree as to the unaided evolution of an alphabet by the Vais.

of the first impression made upon the stranger by Liberia and its inhabitants, our author proceeds to say: " Now, the spectacle that offers itself to the eyes of the visitor is less beautiful.

" It is the spectacle of a nation in decadence.

" And this fact of a nation not yet a century old, which, starting from nothing, raised itself to its apogee in twenty years and has commenced, at the end of barely sixty years, to fall into decay, this fact, I say, deserves that one should pause, for at the first sight it is not natural. And I can only find its explanation in the theory that I attempt to develop here, to wit:

" That the negroes in general and the Liberians in particular are eminently susceptible of perfectionment and progress, but that this perfectionment and this progress are destined to a sudden check, and even to a prompt decadence, if one has sought to orient them in the direction of our European civilization.

" I have said that the spectacle that offers itself to-day to the eyes of the visitor is that of a nation in decadence. In fact the beautiful broad streets cut at the beginning still exist, but they are invaded by vegetation and guttered by deep gullies which

A "CIVILISED" LIBERIAN.

the rain has cut, and which one does not trouble to fill up; the enclosing walls about the different properties are half destroyed without anyone seeking to repair them; a mass of houses in ruin take away from the smiling and attractive aspect of the city; even houses in process of construction are in ruins; a superb college building, erected at great expense upon the summit of the cape, is abandoned, and one permits it to be invaded by the forest and weathered by the rain; the stairway that leads to the upper story of Representatives Hall, having crumbled, has never been reconstructed, and a sort of provisional flight of steps has been for years the only means of access which permits the cabinet officers to enter their offices; the landings waste away stone by stone, and it is difficult to draw boats up to them; the shops where one formerly constructed vessels and landing boats have disappeared; roads, from lack of care, have almost everywhere become native trails again; the plantations of sugar cane and ginger are matters of ancient history, and fields that formerly were well cultivated, have returned to the state of virgin forest; coffee plantations have run wild, choked by the rank vegetation of the tropics. The level of instruction is lowered, the new generations receive only an education of primary grade; of the University of Monrovia, there remains only the name and some mortar board caps which one at times sees upon the heads of professors and candidates.

"All, however, is not dead in the Republic. There is yet a nucleus of Liberians of the ancient time, remarkably instructed and civilized, excellent orators, fine conversationalists, writers of talent.

"There are also among the young people some choice minds who desire to elevate the intellectual and moral level of their country, and who seek to do so by published articles, by lectures, by literary clubs, and by new schools."

Professor Starr comments upon this as follows: "There is much food for thought in these statements of Delafosse. Some of his arraignment is true; on the whole it is less true to-day than when he wrote. There was a period when the Liberians were quite discouraged and things were neglected. Much of this neglect still exists. It would be possible to-day to find houses falling to ruins, crumbling walls, guttered streets, unsatisfactory landing places. But a new energy is rising; the effects of efforts put forth by the nucleus which

Delafosse himself recognizes as existing in Liberia is being felt; contact with the outside world, with its stimulus, sympathies, and friendships, warrants the hope that the future Liberia will surpass the past. We make no attempt to answer Delafosse in detail; in the body of our book most of the questions raised by his remarks are discussed with some fullness."

The hopeful note sounded both by Delafosse and Starr is the result of two terms of presidency and government by the "Nucleus of Liberians of the Ancient time," *circa* 1900 to 1912.

Delafosse's observations were made about 1907, Starr's visit was in 1912, while the present writer was there since these dates, so that we have three independent observers of different nationalities, all friends of African races, and all arriving at the same conclusions with regard to the unsatisfactory progress of the Republic under its Liberio-American rulers. And Liberians of prominence and influence regret the decadence.

Part IV—Home Politics

Not being a politician the present writer depends wholly upon the observation of others for this chapter.

Professor Starr quotes G. W. Ellis as to the decline and fall of the Republican Party and the consequent triumph for years of the so-called "Whig" Party, with the rallying to their banner of those who generally support the Ins against the Outs, and are repaid by the crumbs of Office and jobs that fall from the Government table. Starr comments upon this:

"All this is true, but after all, at the last election there was a considerable awakening of party spirit; it was a bitter political contest. The cry of fraud was loudly raised; seats in Congress were challenged by more than half the total number of membership; the question was seriously asked how an investigation would be possible on account of the lack of unimplicated to conduct it.

INTERNAL CONDITIONS 67

"This outburst of feeling and this cry of fraud came at a bad moment; the nation was appealing for our financial assistance; it was feared that a bad impression might be produced by the condition of disharmony. Under this fear, personal feeling was for the time suppressed and the demand for investigation dropped."

The election Professor Starr refers to was that for the term 1913-16, and the "Nucleus," mentioned by Delafosse, which had undertaken to reform the administration of Justice on the parental advice of the British Government, was beaten at the polls by the means described later on in a quotation from *The African League*.

It was the powers of darkness against the powers of light, and the means by which the former won the battle is interesting as an insight into the desire for power at any price which is the curse of politics in Liberia (as also elsewhere).

Professor Starr says, under the head of "Problems"[1] and the sub-head of "Politics": "There are, however, personal likes and dislikes which will vent themselves in outbursts of party spirit. The last election was really furious. It voiced the local jealousies of the whole Republic.

Just as in the State of Illinois it was Chicago against the counties, and as in New York State it is the City of New York against the up-State districts; so, in Liberia it is Monrovia against the counties. The election was really close after an exciting campaign. Charges of fraud were bitterly advanced. According to *The African League* there were wild doings in Bassa County where it is printed. We refrain from really quoting the *interesting and exciting* passages from its article, but venture to give here its opening paragraphs:

"As the day of the election approached, great preparations were made by the Government and Government officials to defeat the National True Whig Party at any cost, and in any manner. They sent money in every direction to call unqualified nameless bushmen to come, and put into the hands of the Sheriff a paper which is worth only so much gin and rum to the bushmen. These bushmen had never seen, nor heard of, the registrar's office. Neither do they own any land in contemplation of law, but Howard people, simply because they have had the Government's approval in this corruption, had planned to force the corruption into the polls."

And again, " Politics are in great vogue. The

INTERNAL CONDITIONS 69

Liberians never liked work since the establishment of the colony; agriculture even has had but slight attraction for the people. It is not strange, all things considered. The ancestors of these people used to work hard in the fields before they went over there; one reason they went was that they wanted to escape field labour. They had always been accustomed to see their masters live in ease, without soiling their hands with toil; when they became their own masters they naturally wanted to be like the men to whom they had been accustomed to look up to with respect. Trade has always been in high repute. It was easy for the new-comers to trade with the natives of the country and rapidly acquire a competence. So far as work was concerned there were plenty of 'Bush Niggers' to be had cheaply. There is, however, another way of escape from manual labour besides trade—that is professional life. Everywhere people who do not wish to work with their hands may seek a profession; it is so here with us—it is so there with them. The Liberians would rather be 'reverends' or doctors or lawyers than work with their hands.

"Of all the professions, however, law seems to be the favourite. The number of lawyers in Liberia is unnecessarily large, and lawyers naturally drift into politics; they aim to become members of Congress (the Legislature) or judges of the Supreme Court, or members of the Cabinet, or President of the Republic. It is unfortunate that so many of them are anxious for that kind of life, but they are skilled in it, and we have nothing to teach them when it comes to politics.

"We have already said that the Liberians are skilled in politics and that we have but little to teach them. They know quite well what graft means. In fact graft of the finest kind exists and has existed among the native Africans, from time beyond the memory of man. If the Americo-Liberians could have escaped from our own Republic without ideas in this direction, such would quickly have been developed through contact with their native neighbours.

"Unfortunately there is considerable opportunity for graft in the Black Republic. The actual salaries of public officers and congressmen are very small. Important concessions are, however, all the time being demanded by wealthy outside interests. English, German, French, American promoters have always something to propose to that little

Legislature, and they never come with empty hands.

"One of the greatest dangers which the nation faces is found in these great schemes for exploitation offered from outside. The natural resources of the country are very great, but they should be, as far as possible, conserved for the benefit of the people and the nation. The temptation to betray the nation's interest for present personal advantage is always very great."

The chapter upon "Politics" in Professor Starr's work is well worth perusal; in fact the whole of his work can be studied with profitable results by those who desire to see the affairs of the Republic in a true perspective.

Sir Harry Johnston also sums up his criticisms in a kindly spirit, after doing full justice to the intelligence of the Liberian people: "They are quite as well read as the English peasant, are law-abiding, and almost invariably of a kindly disposition. So much for their virtues; and now for their faults or defects, and their mistaken ideals: (1) They are too religious. (2) There is still rather a tendency towards the abuse of alcohol, in which, of course, they are no worse or even a little better than the

Europeans on the west coast of Africa. (3) They are too American in their devotion to frothy oratory and floods of eloquence in print, orations on this subject and on that. Over and over again one is reminded of the American scenes in "Martin Chuzzlewit," as one passes through the coast regions of Liberia. (4) They are too much given up to politics, after the American fashion; and with a zest for unproductive disputation and ridiculous hair-splitting on public questions which gives an American facility for—how shall one phrase it delicately?—making politics more openly a trade than they are yet made in England."

The unsatisfactory elements in the government of Liberia are fundamental. They are mainly due to the fact that instead of the rulers from time to time being the chosen of the people, they are elected by chicanery and force; not by the free will of the citizens of the Republic. Having attained office by these methods, similar action is necessary to enable them to retain their positions, which has led to the present deplorable state of affairs, and will inevitably lead towards a perpetuation of these and other questionable practices to obtain a majority of votes at ensuing elections. Professor Starr has dealt with

INTERNAL CONDITIONS

this subject at length, and, although evidently a reluctant witness, has nevertheless manfully fulfilled the duty of the historian as one who says, " I am in a position to speak the truth, therefore the truth will I speak; impugn it who so lists."

A copy of an appeal to the people around Monrovia, published in the *Government Gazette* for January, 1916, is interesting in that it shows the racial enmity existing between the Liberians and the Kroo people, as well as the lack of firm government on the part of the rulers of the Republic.

> " EXECUTIVE MANSION,
> " MONROVIA.
> " *December* 18*th*, 1915.
>
> " To the Citizens of the St. Paul River in general, and Caldwell, Clay Ashland, Virginia, White Plains, and Crozierville in particular.
>
> " FELLOW CITIZENS,—I regret to inform you that I have heard very unpleasant reports of the actions of certain of my fellow-citizens towards that portion of our citizenship in your midst composed of Kroo people.
>
> " They have complained to me of threats having been made on their lives by citizens in Caldwell,

whose names were given to me, that if they were found out after six o'clock p.m. they would be shot; also, that violence has been done to their property in the settlements specifically named, all of which is said to be done in retaliation for the alleged killing in Virginia, supposed to have been done by the Kroos.

"I have to remind you that the Kroos who were accused of the killing in Virginia were tried and acquitted in our own court by a jury composed mostly, if not entirely, of persons from the River.

"I am already overburdened with the responsibility of dealing with the acts of unthinking and irresponsible persons, and have to warn you one and all, good loyal citizens, to raise your voice and lend your aid against any and everything that savours of lawlessness. By so doing you avert the bringing of trouble and the frown of God upon your country, which every citizen is, by his lone actions, capable of doing.

"It is worse than hypocrisy to pray in our churches for God to bring in the native people and then deny them the benefit of the law of the land for which we contend so strongly.

"The law, of course, will be rigidly enforced upon violaters without partiality, but I feel that all good and law-abiding citizens should be sufficiently interested in the good name of their townships to see that it is not defamed by reckless persons, and I take this method of calling upon such persons to maintain the dignity of the State and the Constitution which guarantees to all men the right to enjoy life, liberty, and to defend his property.

"Your obedient servant,
"D. E. HOWARD,
"*President, R.L.*"

The lives of the Kroos having been threatened and their property "violated" by certain persons whose names were given in their complaint and appeal for justice, the President publishes a homily on the duty of good citizens, instead of issuing a warrant for the arrest of the offenders against the law and the Constitution.

The following extracts are given from *The African Mail* of April 7th, 1916.

"Our well-informed Liberian correspondent sends us a disquieting communication by the last mail. In point of fact, so grave are some of the allegations that we have hesitated to publish them.

"What remains of his letter is serious enough as readers will see for themselves. The charge of being Germanic in their sympathies is laid against the Government. Certainly there would appear to be some reason for this if the statements we hear from various sources are to be relied upon. 'There is no smoke without fire.' We have upon many occasions given publicity to articles sympathetic towards Liberia in the crises she has passed through, but her present position is apparently of her own creation, and we are led to believe was easily avoidable. It has never been our policy to allow anybody and everybody with an axe to grind the hospitality of our columns, and despite the remarks made in a Liberian newspaper some time ago, we have not departed from our rule now. The indictments we have not printed are very much worse than anything we have. Presidents of Liberia have never occupied a bed of roses, and the present holder of the office has one of thorns. Probably the worst of all State troubles are internecine ones, and those are very much in evidence in the little West African Republic. The Administration appears to have run

INTERNAL CONDITIONS 77

riot, and plunged the ship of State into a maelström from which there will be considerable difficulty in securing release.

"A strong hand is wanted at the helm, but the term does not necessarily imply a hand that brooks no interference with its personal control. The next election may see a change for the better. Let us hope so. We should very much like to see Liberia emerge triumphantly through all her troubles by her own efforts, but we are afraid that, if matters are allowed to go on as they are, her real safety will lie in the absolute security afforded by the overlordship of the country by an outside Power."

The communication referred to, only part of which is published, is entitled, "Excitement and Gloom in Liberia," "Special to *The African Mail*."

The West African Republic was in the throes of excitement in 1915-16. The Kroos on the Sinoe coast rose in rebellion, and succeeded in cutting off communication by sea between Sinoe and the rest of the Republic, their war canoes blockading the ports. The Liberian Government appealed to the American Government for help, and the cruiser *Chester* came to these waters. The "Liberian Frontier Force" (the paid police), under a black American Captain, sent by the United States Government in connection with the American loan negotiations, defeated the Kroos with great slaughter in several battles. But the Kroos also did some deadly work; in January, 1915, they captured a sail boat flying the Liberian flag, and killed twelve of its occupants, one being a last year's graduate of the Liberian College, a young man of great promise.

Liberian Government regarded as Pro-German

President Howard created the impression abroad that his administration was under German influence. Secretary King[1] was given a state luncheon in Berlin in July, 1914, a few weeks before the war began, and many a rumour was current as to what occurred then. A serious controversy arose with the British Government with reference to the conduct of the Germans in Liberia soon after the war broke out, and Secretary King was charged by the Allies with favouring the German side. In his annual message the then President so offended the Allies that, when he was inaugurated (taking office for his last term of four years), the British Consul

---

[1] Since twice elected President (the last time in 1923).

INTERNAL CONDITIONS 79

was not present, nor was the French Consul, and what was more significant, not a single representative of Allied business interests was present, the occasion being marked only by the smiling faces of the German residents. There was some sentiment strongly in favour of the cause of the Allies, but unfortunately Liberians are not much given to independent speaking. One man spoke out and the Government put him in jail without bail, and a woman was held without bail for "talking too much." In each case it was an "ally" who got caught. No wonder everybody shut up like a clam.[1]

A Gloomy Outlook

The Liberian Government is without money to pay its running expenses. It is really hard on men with families; yet such is their patriotism that no one grumbles seriously. But how long such a state of things can last it is difficult to tell. One thing is certain, ways and means will have to be devised to get out of this tangle.

[1] Since the above was written matters have changed greatly. Liberia eventually declared with the Allies, and the French cable station at Monrovia was bombarded by a German cruiser.

American Government's Assistance

The American Legation has taken a direct hand in the management of things, and has accomplished some results, as the Secretary of Legation is in close touch with the President. It is pathetic to hear some of the " street corner talks," recalling " the good old days."

CHAPTER III

ADMINISTRATION OF JUSTICE

Part I—General

THE administration of Justice at headquarters in Monrovia is, in a measure, not much different from that in other communities where the lawyer-politician is in the ascendant, and the client with the most money or political influence obtains the best, or the least scrupulous, advocate, as the case may require.

There is a trite English story of an answer given to an appellant by the Master of the Rolls. During a session of his Court a lady rushed impulsively forward with clasped hands in the recognized dramatic manner, and exclaimed: " My Lord, I demand justice."

A whimsical expression flitted over the conventional judicial pose of his Lordship's features as he answered the appeal: " I am exceedingly sorry to say, Madam, that you have come to the wrong shop. Here we only deal in Law."

When this was the attitude of one of our most learned Judges in what we Englishmen have long regarded as the hub of the Universe as far as the administration of Justice is concerned, which of us would be entitled to cast a stone at the little Liberian Republic if her conceptions of Justice were to fall short of even that standard.

Therefore the " Administration of the Law " might have been the title of this chapter, for although the layman presumes that Law and Justice are one the lawyer knows them to be widely apart.

The delegation of the administration of Justice to small farmers or residents in the suburbs of the capital, who, as J.P.s represent the " Great Unpaid " of our own organization, is at the root of all the evils that fall upon the residents and the natives in the outer districts of the Settlements, where the employer of labour is in litigation with and sues the employee or vice versâ. With us J.P.s are unpaid, because they are generally men of high standing in the county or town, and are, moreover, unpaid by their own desire, as they prefer to occupy a position of honour without emoluments which would detract from the merit of their service to the community, and to the nation.

In Liberia, of course, there are few whose income is independent of their daily work; yet the desire to rule over their fellow men, and lay down the law from the bench, is even more insistent than amongst ourselves. The appointment to the position of Justice of the Peace is, as a rule, the result of political support of some candidate for office at elections, and in the Liberian Press references and implications have been made on this subject without raising a question of prosecution for slander, or for bribery and corruption; so that one may accept the idea that, at least, it is not unusual for political support to be recompensed by elevation to the bench, or to a higher office.

Now these "gauds" are what men strive for in the world as it is at present, and were it not for the disastrous results affecting the native population surrounding the seats of Justice, due to the appointment of law-givers for other reasons than that of uprightness of character, independence of spirit, honesty of purpose, and all other virtues that should qualify a man who is set in authority over his fellow man, there would be very little difference between the Liberian methods of appointing Solons and those of more civilized communities nearer home.

But in the latter case the J.P. is, as a rule, dealing with a free and enlightened fellow subject, who knows that his remedy for an unjust ruling lies in appeal to a higher authority; while the native subject of Liberia (with the exception, of course, of the Liberio-American race) knows no law, and, being accustomed to the autocratic rule of his own chiefs, takes the decision of the J.P. as final, although, because the instinct of Justice is inherent in even the most untutored races of mankind, he may know that the decision is unjust.

As a matter of fact, and of common knowledge, the political factor enters into every judiciary appointment, from the J.P. to the Chief Justice; and the highest appointment forms a convenient side line on which a dangerous rival to the presidential chair is frequently shunted. Perhaps a still more vital objection to the existing system, and one which is fatal to the purity of the stream of Justice flowing from the Liberian Courts, lies in the practice of lower judicial functionaries paying themselves out of the fees and fines of the Court. This practice leads to trivial charges against individuals, adjournments, and other devices to lengthen out proceedings which are producing the funds, on the system

ADMINISTRATION OF JUSTICE

of the more work the more pay, and the higher the fines the more money passing through the Court.

The subordinate officers of the Court are on the same pay roll, and if any of the Fees of Court reach the Treasury at all they are only the bare charges laid down by regulation, which, therefore, have to be accounted for in the periodical returns of the proceedings.

In this direction also, there is the temptation to make each case contribute to the pay roll of the Court, and the decision is generally against the man of substance who is able to pay both fees and fines, with but little regard to the abstract justice of the case in hand.

Another contributory source of the revenues of the J.P. lies in the fact that the African is inherently fond of litigation, which takes the place of the " palavers " in his tribal life, and hales his neighbour before a magistrate on the slightest personal provocation, as well as for small debts. It is a satisfaction to him, whether he wins his case or not, even if it costs him more than the original claim, for he has had his day out, haranguing the Bench, or listening to his advocate doing so on his behalf.

It frequently happens that the defendant cannot pay the debt and the costs, so that, as imprisonment for debt still holds in Liberia, he is thrown into jail until he can do so, a course now more or less obsolete elsewhere.

In cases where the State prosecutes and the culprit is convicted, he is fined, perhaps with the alternative of imprisonment, and if he is unable to pay the fine and Court expenses, although officially in prison, he is actually working on the farm of the magistrate or some other functionary.

When the term of his sentence is approaching its conclusion the prisoner is frequently charged with some trivial breach of the regulations, for which he is sentenced to another fine or a further term of imprisonment. More often so when the season of farm work is in full swing, and hired labour is scarce and costly.

Some examples of the travesty of Justice in the country districts, one of which nearly had a tragic ending, came under my own notice while in the Interior.

My " Head Boy," Lamin, was party to a brawl in one of the camps.

One of the camp bullies was interfering with his

ADMINISTRATION OF JUSTICE 87

friend's wife, and as the husband was not strong enough to give the man a thrashing, Lamin intervened and did it for him.

The result was a summons before the magistrate, and an absence of nearly a week from his work; and when he returned he was a sick man, having been poisoned, probably by a Witch Doctor, at the instigation, or in the employ of, his opponent.

The farcical part of the proceedings was that the prosecutor was fined and charged for expenses of serving summons over ten dollars, while my steward, the defendant, had been fined about thirteen dollars, and the husband of the woman was also fined, although he was only a witness in the case, for yawning, coughing and sneezing in the Court. Lamin's pay was ten dollars a month, and the other two were labourers at one shilling a day.

The brawl was insignificant, but the fines and loss of time to the boys amounted to over a month's pay for each of the parties, while a greater loss fell upon the innocent employers. A British Commissioner's Court would have dismissed the case, as the complainant was the first offender, or have fined Lamin five shillings at the utmost.

Lamin lay for weeks in the town fighting for his

life, and the charge of poisoning was laid against the other man. The authorities sent to inquire into the case. Nothing came of it, however, although all the town knew that the bully was boasting of his crime. But Witch Doctors are uncanny people to deal with in the Bush of Liberia.

These " palavers " were continually happening, to the annoyance and loss of the employers, who, if they wanted their servant to return, had to advance the money to pay the fines.

Another failure of Justices' justice happened about the same date.

The loss of some stores, tents, etc., caused an inquiry which resulted in their discovery at a small town in the Bush, and the charge of stealing them was laid against a former employee of the firm.

Two constables visited the town in question and found the articles in the house of the accused, but the thief had got wind of their coming and bolted to the Bush. The constables tried to take the stolen goods, but the man's friends drove them out of the town with violence, and they returned to report their failure.

The firm was charged the expenses, but refused

ADMINISTRATION OF JUSTICE 89

to pay them unless the man was caught and the goods returned, whereupon a fresh visit was made to the town and the man was brought down in custody. He was taken before the magistrate charged with the theft; was committed, and sent to jail pending trial. The jailer, however, let him go, on his own responsibility, probably bribed to do so. The firm appealed to headquarters for Justice, whereupon the constables were sent forth a third time, and, of course, the thief had disappeared with the stolen property into the "High Bush," where no Liberian would dare to follow.

Trivial matters, perhaps, but directly affecting the lives, liberty, and property of both Europeans and natives under the Government of Liberia.

On a larger scale the ingenious idea of fining both parties to a quarrel is applied to tribal chiefs.

When the quarrel is a serious one, and likely to spread into larger issues, a "Commissioner" is detailed to go and hear the "palaver" and act as arbitrator.

If the scene is far from the coast the Commissioner requires a large escort, and the writer has met thirty to forty native soldiers, with their carriers, following a Liberian Commissioner up country. As the expedition lives upon the country they pass through they are not welcomed by the towns or people, because they are given to commandeering anything that they fancy.

I am told that the proceedings at the trial are more or less a farce, and that the finding is generally that both sides are in the wrong, so both are fined, either in dollars, cattle, or produce, to pay the costs of the expedition and the fees of the Commissioner, whose decision is something like this:

"A. you are in the right to a certain degree, but you are in the wrong also because you took up arms without authority of the Government, you are therefore fined two hundred dollars. B. you were wrong in attacking A. without first reporting the matter to the Government, so you must find the same amount as A."

As both sides are dissatisfied, and moreover wish to resume their quarrel as soon as the soldiers have left, the produce or cows are paid and the army departs laden with spoil.

The countryside is also glad to get rid of the soldiers so that their men, who have been hiding in the Bush to avoid being taken as carriers, may come

ADMINISTRATION OF JUSTICE

back to their towns. They hasten the parting guest gladly, and the expedition returns, having accomplished nothing in the way of administering Justice, but with the spoils of victory as of a successful raid into an enemy's country.

Part II—Justice in Theory

From a study of the subject it is found that the judiciary system, originally copied from that of the United States, bears in some respects a resemblance to our own.

The initial process is before a Justice of the Peace, before whose Court persons charged with an offence against the laws are brought for examination. They may waive the action of this Court, that is, reserve their defence, and bail is immediately fixed.

If bail is found, they are free until the case comes before the Grand Jury, but if they cannot find bail they go to jail pending the action of the Grand Jury. In cases where the Grand Jury throws out the charge, or in cases where, after two sittings of the same body, no indictment is framed against the accused, he is released from custody, or bail, as the case may be.

The J.P. has jurisdiction also over civil cases, claims for debt, damages for trespass, and other

ADMINISTRATION OF JUSTICE

causes, if the amount does not exceed ten pounds, and as these causes affect the great mass of the people who appeal to his tribunal for Justice, the administration requires honest, intelligent, and impartial magistrates.

Sad to say, the reverse of this desired qualification for authority holds sway in Liberia, for in most instances, as before stated, the appointments are filled by petty politicians who seek the appointment from the President as a reward for political services, and who regard their high office simply as a money-making concern.

Generally speaking the J.P. is a public plunderer, subservient to the political party of the hour, and in many cases without the slightest knowledge of either Law or the ethics of Justice.

They swarm like flies over that part of the Republic in which their lives are safe, so that a litigant may pick and choose between two or three J.P.'s within a radius of two miles, but there is little choice on the score of impartiality, and it would be a rare occurrence for a native to obtain judgment against an Americo-Liberian, or for a white man to succeed against either of them, because, as exemplified in another place, the judgment is invariably against the longest purse to ensure the payment of fees, costs, and the revenue of the J.P.

Of course the litigants have the right of appeal to what is called the Monthly Court because it meets once a month. It is combined with the Probate Court and has civil jurisdiction under the administration of one Judge up to forty pounds.

Above this there is the Circuit Court, one for each of the four counties, meeting quarterly and having unlimited civil and criminal jurisdiction. This Court forms the Appeal Court for the lower courts, and has a Grand Jury as well as petty juries, somewhat similar to the system in both England and America, and these juries practically hold power over the issues concerning the property, the liberty, and the lives of the people.

A PALAVER WITH CHIEFS, UPPER LIBERIA (FRANCO-BRITISH FRONTIERS)

Part III—Justice in Practice

Although similar in constitution to our Courts theoretically, in practice the operation of the jury system is farcical.

The political "Boss" in each town has as his perquisite the right to nominate a certain number of jurors for each term of the sittings of the Court, and usually appoints his political henchmen, and is thus able to control the course of Justice. He moreover, is able to reward his supporters for their services, as they are paid by the fees for jurors, during the session.

If any issue is before the Court affecting the political "Bosses," the political machinery is started to guide and control the findings of both Judge and Jury. Many members of the Legislature are lawyers (gaining admission to the Bar without efficient examination) not because of their knowledge of Law, but because they are members of the Legislature. Because the Legislature has the right to remove the Judges upon petition to the President with cause stated, or by impeachment, these Lawyer-Legislators threaten Judges with removal if they decide cases against them, or disobey the orders of the political " Bosses."

The final Court of Appeal from the other Courts, and the highest seat of Law and Justice in the land, is the Supreme Court. This Court sat once a year in former times, but when judicial reform was suggested by Great Britain in 1907, and the necessity for improvement was supported by a small but influential section of the community who were well aware of the faults of their system in this direction, the necessary act was passed providing for two terms a year, and thrown as a sop to Cerberus; but there the reforms stopped short, as far as any purifying influence from the abuses above indicated are concerned.

It will be recognized from the foregoing that while the system of administration of Justice in Liberia is excellent in theory, in practice it constitutes an ever-present danger to the people of the country, and especially to those who are ignorant of their rights as citizens, and also of the Law itself, as well as to foreigners with their invested interests. Even white American friends of Liberia distrust the

ADMINISTRATION OF JUSTICE 97

Judiciary. An application was made a few years ago by an influential American group for a railway and timber concession, but with the stipulation that all controversies arising under the concession must be submitted to and tried in the Federal Courts of America.

The weakness of the Judiciary arises not only from the want of good Judges but also from the fact that one can count upon the fingers of one hand the trained lawyers at the Bar, and they are chiefly from American Law Schools, with diplomas varying from the highest down to a non-committal certificate of the period of study.

It may be truly said that well trained lawyers are the life-blood of the Courts, as the Judges come from among them; and it is to be regretted that there are no educational facilities for training the local lawyers who swarm in Liberia. Again, in theory, the wise men of old had provided for this need by establishing a Chair in the College of Liberia, and a professor is maintained at a salary comparatively handsome, but he seldom meets his classes. It was alleged against a recent incumbent that he only attended on three occasions in one year, and yet drew his salary in addition to that of another high office in the Government. There are no lectures, therefore, in Constitutional, Civil, or Criminal Law; the teaching being, generally speaking, confined to the Liberian Statutes, with an occasional reference to out-of-date text-books.

If a candidate acquires a little superficial knowledge of this pabulum, and, moreover, has the necessary political pull, he is admitted to the Bar, and begins to practise upon the unfortunate public forthwith.

Having taken "stuff" these budding legal luminaries have to live, so that inducing litigation is one of the lightest charges to be made against their methods, while, with an exception here and there, they are not above taking retainers from both sides, or changing from one to the other and supporting the heaviest purse. In fact, they are parasites upon the community. As remarked before the African races are extremely fond of litigation, and regard a day in the Courts as an amusement, a red letter day, so that the parasites prey upon the public sufficiently to make a lining to a black coat, which is naturally the highest ambition to those born below the rank of the Aristocracy of the Robe.

Given time, with the gift of speech, and a political

shove, these barristers later on fill the higher offices of the Courts, but still run with the hare and hunt with the hounds in some cases. It is alleged against an Attorney-General holding office not many years ago, that while acting for Government he took a fee from the party against whom he was supposed to be proceeding on behalf of the Government.

Again a step higher, and from the same men, as we have said, the Judges are selected. It is not, therefore, in any way surprising that the British Government as foster-father informed the President of the Republic in 1907, " That the Judiciary must be reformed, as an ignorant and corrupt Judiciary is intolerable."

Part IV—Reformation

The President of the day took the lesson to heart and declared his intention to make radical changes in the Judiciary so as to improve its "personnel," and, moreover, to free the administration of Justice from political influence. Above all, he proposed to use the knife and cut out the cancer of corruption which was poisoning the body corporate.

He was vigorously supported with fearlessness and energy by a small element led by one of the leading lawyers, a man of the highest ideals and world-wide experience; the only lawyer with College and University Diplomas, and the Certificate of the Highest Court of the United States of America, who had adopted Liberia as his home, and had become a naturalized citizen. The President subsequently appointed him to the Supreme Court in order to commence the purgation, and in 1909 this Judge delivered an address before the Liberian Bar Association on "The Impartial Administration of

ADMINISTRATION OF JUSTICE 101

Justice," which was printed and circulated freely throughout the Republic. The Chair was occupied by the then Vice-President of the Republic (afterwards Chief Justice), who had formerly served as an Associate Judge of the Supreme Court for ten years. The following sweeping indictment was formulated by the Judge against the Bar and the Courts of the Republic. " Gentlemen of the Bar: can we be quiet while our Judges are charged both at home and abroad with (1) ignorance; (2) excessive use of intoxicants; (3) the exhibition of prejudice or passion in the trial of causes; (4) shocking immorality; (5) accepting retainers from private parties; (6) sharing moneys offered as a reward for the arrest of criminals; (7) accepting bribes? "

In the same address is found a quotation from the President's annual message to the Legislature a year before (December, 1908).

" I want to emphasize the fact that there is considerable discontent with reference to our judicial administration. I have had filed in my office during the last twelve months complaints against every Judge of the Court of Quarter Sessions and Common Pleas in the country, besides two against Judges of the Monthly Court and Probate Court.

All these complaints were not well founded, but it is a symptom of which we ought to take notice."

It will be seen from these quotations that the President and his supporters had taken the kindly advice of the British Government seriously to heart, and were fearless in their statement of the existing evils. Before the end of the President's term of office an endeavour was made to at least mitigate some of the evils by the introduction to the Legislature, and the enactment of a partial measure of Judiciary reform; so some prospect of improvement in the administration of Justice appeared above the horizon.

Part V—In Retrogression

The successor to the Presidency took office in 1913, and, being opposed to the party of reform, not only failed to carry out the provisions of the above measure, but pursued a policy which resulted in bringing the Judiciary under the power of his own political party, in defiance of the Constitution, under which the fundamental powers and independence of that department presented an obstacle to his desire for supreme power. Instead of leaving the supervision of the Judiciary to the Chief Justice and the Supreme Court he sought to subvert that authority by giving the Judges to understand, both by personal contact and by formal conferences, that they must work in harmony with the Executive, and enforced his views by paying them their salaries, or withholding them, or by delaying them, through his Secretary to the Treasury, according to their readiness or otherwise to give their submission to the political suggestions of working " in harmony with the Executive."

That the President's party had fully "collared the machine" may be illustrated by the tactics pursued when he was standing for election. An Associate Justice of the Supreme Court gave a decision which the President's political party deemed injurious to the chances of his election. As certain charges could be brought against the Judge in question these were formulated, and the political followers of the new President (then Secretary of the Treasury) clamoured for the removal of the Judge from the Bench. This was easily accomplished, as the Candidate for the Presidential Chair still held on to the Treasury which made him the most powerful member of a Government, whose funds were generally short, and where paying went by favour. After the election of the President the Legislature tried and exonerated the Judge in question, but the President ignored that finding, and declined to allow him to return to the Bench of the Supreme Court. He then endeavoured to force the Judge to resign, but, failing in this, the President offered him an office outside the Judiciary which the Judge declined, so the President appointed a political adherent to be Associate Justice, and notified the Supreme

ADMINISTRATION OF JUSTICE 105

Court that he had appointed him in place of the recalcitrant Judge, who was "suspended." At the next sitting of the Court a military guard was placed at the door and the Judge, who would not bow to the Executive, was prevented by force from taking his seat on the Bench, and there the matter ended.

Another instance of the perversion of the Constitution in endeavouring to control the Judiciary is furnished by the President's treatment of another Judge, whose independence and support of the policy of reform made him a thorn in the side of the Executive. Without any special controversy between the Judge and the President or the Legislature, and without any charges being formulated or cause stated, and, moreover, without notice, but after holding a secret canvass of the Legislature, the President was able to pass through the Legislature an Act giving him the power to remove the Justice from the Bench of the Supreme Court, and to appoint another in his place. This Act was passed within three hours from the time of its introduction.

Anything more pernicious than such an Act can hardly be conceived; and it is alleged that even in

Liberia the passing of such a measure was only made possible by the subordination of the leaders of parties in the Legislature by promises of promotion to the vacancy created by the removal and nominations to other offices.

The Constitution of Liberia provides that the judicial power of the Republic shall be vested in one Supreme Court, and such subordinate Courts as the Legislature may from time to time establish. The Judges of the Supreme Court and all other Judges of Courts shall hold office during good behaviour, but may be removed by the President on the address of two-thirds of both Houses, the cause being stated, or by impeachment. In this latter case the Judge in question vigorously contested the validity of the Act by challenging both the President and Legislature to state the cause of their action, and by a motion before his own Court, but without success, as the Supreme Court, being thoroughly cowed, declined to give any decision; on the other hand an armed constabulary was employed to prevent the Judge from entering the Court Room. The President, who thus overrode the very Constitution by which he held office, was elected for a second term of office; and it is a sad

ADMINISTRATION OF JUSTICE

commentary on his administration that while the Constitution provides for a Chief Justice and two Associate Justices, there should have been four of the latter, two sitting by appointment to seats which were not vacant, and two prevented from sitting, and set aside from their high office, practically by force of arms, and without the warrant of the Law.

CHAPTER IV

THE LIBERTY OF THE SUBJECT

Part I—General Definitions of Slavery

IT may be assumed that it was in order to escape from the horrors of slavery, and to establish an asylum for all others who could escape therefrom, that the New Pilgrim Fathers crossed the Atlantic and founded the Liberian Settlement in 1822. At that period slavery, that is the buying and selling of one race of men by another more powerful, was still recognized in the United States, although importation had been checked, and the process of repatriation had been begun by Great Britain. Later on, when the Settlement became a State, in 1847, the Constitution adopted laid down in Article I, Declaration of Rights, under Section 4, that: "There shall be no slavery within this Republic; nor shall any person resident therein deal in slaves either within or without this Republic."

It was due to these principles that the early Mission was protected by passing warships of other Powers in patrolling the West African coast, and, moreover, it is abundantly proved in the history of the Settlement that but for this protection and other material assistance the early settlers would have been stranded, or driven into the sea, on several occasions.

Later on, in 1847, when a Republic was proclaimed, it was that outstanding rock, on which the Constitution was founded, the absolute prohibition of slavery throughout the Republic, which led Great Britain, and afterwards other great Powers who had acknowledged their sins in slave dealing, to recognize the new State; for they had also taken the best possible measures to recompense the African races for their sins in the past, and to ensure that in the future, wherever possible under their flags, slavery should be abolished in Africa, and elsewhere throughout the world. They, therefore, welcomed the coming of the new element in the regeneration of Africa, and have continued to extend to the Republic sympathetic care and advice for close upon a century, from the first settlement, and sixty years of constitutional government, relying

THE LIBERTY OF THE SUBJECT 111

chiefly upon the theoretically benevolent attitude of the rulers toward the native tribes, that justice would be done, and that the ideals of the founders of the State would be eventually carried into effect.

The extirpation of slavery has been thoroughly carried out by most of the Colonizing Powers in Africa, and especially in the British and French Colonies; but it was only after many little wars and continual pressure on the Chiefs, who bitterly resented the interference of Europeans with a practice inherent in African and Asiatic races which has existed from the days of the Biblical Patriarchs. Slavery in all its forms contributed largely to the revenues of Chiefs, and, moreover, to their prestige; because wealth and rank were expressed by the number of slaves as well as cattle, sheep, horses, and other worldly goods which represented the silver and gold of modern times in other communities.

British ideas of slavery in the last century were mainly drawn from what we now know to be a purposely overdrawn picture. The slave bowed down with a hard taskmaster standing over him armed with a heavy whip, as exemplified in Uncle

Tom's Cabin, with Legree in the rôle of chief villain. Such cruelty, of course, was, and is still, possible, but exceptional; and some kinds of what is still misnamed " slavery " constitute in the main a comparatively happy life in Africa.

There are degrees of course. In former times, when the slave had been snatched from his native town and separated from his wife, parents, and children, marched hundreds of miles through forest, or across deserts, to the port, only to suffer deeper misery on the voyage to a strange Continent whence he was never to return, it would probably sum up the greatest amount of agony that can be crowded into one short human life. In West Africa, however, there are three kinds of slaves, or more properly speaking there were; and a personal experience will show clearly the worst type.

It is only a little over twenty years ago that the present writer was called into the compound of a Chief in a large fortified town of Senegambia.

The object of my visit was to doctor the Chief's brother, who was thought to be dying. Standing stark naked in the compound, in the glaring,

VILLAGE AND NATIVES, LIBERIAN INTERIOR.

THE LIBERTY OF THE SUBJECT

blistering sunshine stood a slave, heavily ironed, with a fragment of the connecting chain of the march still attached. A caravan from the Niger valley had passed that morning and the man represented the Chief's commission or " dash " for safe conduct through his territory. The work that I was then engaged on would not allow of interference, as its success depended upon the goodwill of the Chiefs, and, moreover, I had no armed force with the expedition, so that I could not have enforced any order for release. I managed to obtain the slave, however, a day or two afterwards, when the Chief sent me a valuable horse in recognition of having saved his brother's life, which I exchanged for the slave on the score that I could not guard the horse from tsetse fly in camp, and, therefore, would prefer the slave I had seen when I doctored his brother.

This most damnable form of slavery is now a thing of the past in our Colonies and in those of the French; a modified form appears to still exist in some of the Portuguese territories in South-West Africa; while some of the " Regulations " under which the Germans procured their native labour may be classed as somewhat similar, that is to say, paying a Chief to hand over fifty or a hundred of his people permanently. Although carried out officially, and in due form, this is an infraction of the principles of freedom, and should be classed as slavery.

There is another class of so-called slavery which entails no hardship upon the individual; it is called " domestic slavery," and is simply the continuation of Patriachal rule which has existed among these and other Asio-Afric peoples since the days of Abraham, and probably for all time back to the days when marriage was unknown and all children of the tribe had equal rights. These domestic slaves are the children of bondswomen, and are seldom, if ever, sold, though they may be pawned for a term of years to pay off by their service a debt owing by their fathers or Chiefs.

Speaking generally, among the tribes of the Interior, there is a very thin line drawn between these and the children of the legitimate wife or wives; and in some cases the son or daughter of the head of the family, by a bondwoman, becomes the favourite child, and the boy may grow up to supersede the legitimate heir when the time comes for a new Chief.

THE LIBERTY OF THE SUBJECT

There will be no more domestic slavery in British territories after the present generation has died off, as from a certain date (now some years back) all natives born under our flag were made free by proclamation: this will, however, only slightly alter family life, as freedom from his family ties is the last thing an African desires. On the other hand, he sacrifices a great deal in many parts of Africa in order to revisit his family periodically, and so retain his tribal and other rights and privileges.

Another form of semi-slavery which it is more difficult to control is that known as "pawning." Where the pawn is of mature age and pledges himself to relieve his family from debt there may be little objection to the practice, as he simply sells his labour for a lump sum instead of a wage, and in other forms it is common to all nations; but where the pawn is of tender age, and has no idea of the transaction which hampers his future, there is but little to divide it from the worst forms of traffic in human blood. Female children especially should be protected from this evil, for although later on they are practically sold into marriage (which is practically not an unusual occurrence even in more civilized communities) they still have, if free, a large say in choosing a husband, while the pawn has none.

An example of this form of slavery came to the writer's knowledge during his residence in Liberia. The head boy of the house in which he was staying came to tell his master that there was a man outside who wanted to sell a boy. On inquiry it was found that the boy's father was in prison for debt, and his relatives wished to pawn the boy for the amount of the debt (then stated to be four pounds), so that his father could be released.

This amount was forthcoming, and the boy was taken on to the farm to work out his own salvation as well as his father's.

The relatives of the boy returned next day to say that the charges now amounted to five pounds thirteen shillings on account of the additional charge of the court and jail for releasing the prisoner. The additional amount was also paid, and the father released.

Possibly there are other cases where the pawn becomes an apprentice and repays the debt by his own work, but even then any transaction of this nature affecting the liberty of a subject should be under the control of Government.

THE LIBERTY OF THE SUBJECT

The foregoing explanation of the different forms of slavery in West Africa, past and present, is necessary to those unacquainted with the subject, in order that they may thoroughly understand the gravity of the charges made against the past and present rulers of the Liberian Republic.

Part II—*Hiring out Kroo-boys*

The hiring out of Kroo-boys by the Government of Liberia is a matter of common knowledge on the West African coast, and perhaps in the circumstances there is little fault to be found with the principle, as the gentle Kroo-boy is far and away the best labourer to be found, and is especially good in the working of ships and boats, for which purpose our own nation has been party to the custom, both in naval and merchant ships. Where a Government is consistently face to face with an empty Treasury it may be forced into the hiring out of some of its subjects, even while its own territory requires the labour of every able-bodied man for its industrial development.

But the methods adopted in Liberia to raise revenue from this source leave much to be desired in the interests of the Kroo labourers.

Instead of adequate measures to guide and regulate the expatriation and return of the backbone of the country, which would control the emigration by

THE LIBERTY OF THE SUBJECT

allowing it in certain districts where labour is plentiful, and veto it in those where able-bodied men are scarce, so providing for the development of home industries, the right of hiring out is let by contract to an alien firm which charges the hirer so much "Head Money," and shares the proceeds with the Government. The more men shipped the more dollars both for the contractor and for the Treasury, and if it were not for the strong affection of the Kroo people for what they call "We Country," which brings them back once a year in order to comply with their own tribal laws, the Kroo coast would be depopulated, as were other parts of West Africa in the days of tribal wars and slavery in its worst form.

The Treasury also benefits in a secondary way by a condition in the contract with the employer at other ports on the coast under which part of the wages for the year's service must be paid in merchandise; so, when the Kroo-boy returns to his own country he is charged import duties upon his goods, and as he is unable to purchase them in bond, he thus pays the import duty to the Colony he works in, the trade profit to his employer in that country (which, with freight and duty added, is generally an enhancement of about fifty per cent. on the prime cost), and finally further duty to his own Government, which in the writer's experience is also heavy, so that in the end the returned labourer has but little profit on the one-half of his year's work.

Formerly "Boys" could be taken off, from their own beach, under a contract with the Chief of their tribe, but now the embarkation and return must be made at one of the several Customs ports on the Liberian coast under heavy penalties on shipmasters, so the net is drawn fairly fine. To an amphibian like the Kroo-boy, the mile or two of sea separating a ship's deck from his native village, when passing, is a trifle, and he occasionally takes French leave in those circumstances, and pushing his trade box before him swims until picked up by a canoe. His relations meet him on the beach, and in accordance with native custom his seniors help themselves to a goodly share of his trade, so that he gains but little in the end either way by his love of home and country and often decides to make his home elsewhere, e.g., the Kroo Colonies at Sierra Leone and other ports.

Part III—Traffic in Native Subjects

A transaction in Liberia of another nature, only differing slightly from the worst form of slavery, may be noted here. The information occurs in the report of a reliable plantation manager of which the following is a verbatim copy:

" I have nothing of a satisfactory nature to convey by this opportunity *re* future labour for the estate. Chiefs Gangawoo and Blama, for whom I sent a canoe down to Monrovia on Thursday last at their request, sent word back that they could not come to see me until the end of this week, or the beginning of next, as they had not finished their palavers with the Government. I had, however, a visit on the 31st January from King Mulba and his suite. He is the Chief of the Belli Tribe, and he promised us about 50 boys as soon as the farming season was over, viz., next month. I do not, however, place much reliance on this Chief's promise as I understand he cannot command many labourers; his visit may, however, do some good as he was well treated here —with a few bottles of gin and some tobacco—with which he expressed great satisfaction. I learnt from him the reason of his and other Chiefs' (over 50 in number) visits to Monrovia, which are as follows:—

"1. The Government have for the past year or more, and without giving any notice, pounced upon the tribal Chiefs for hut and other taxes; they having had no time to prepare payment for these claims in kind, the officials sent up, under escort of a detachment of the Liberian Frontier Force, not only confiscated their cattle, grain, etc., but brought down as hostages numbers of their boys who were relegated to work, for no payment, on the Liberian Coffee Estates for some time, then shipped to Fernando Po, for which the Liberian Government receive £5 per head head-money from the Spanish Government. I sent a Liberian Overseer down to Monrovia to verify this, and he tells me that he has seen statistics showing that in 1915 no less than 2,000 boys were shipped to Fernando Po from Monrovia alone!

"2. King Mulba also told me that the carriers

THE LIBERTY OF THE SUBJECT

he had sent down to Liberian Settlements on the St. Paul's River, and to Monrovia, to dispose of his rice had never returned to their country, and that presumably they had also been taken by the Government or their agents for shipment.

"These are the grievances of the native Chiefs from the Interior, and as they are not satisfied with the result of their interviews with Government they are determined not to permit their subjects to go anywhere near Monrovia or other Liberian Settlements, at least until their palavers are satisfactorily settled. Chief Mulba told me that he and other Chiefs had not now sufficient boys to build their towns or to work their farms owing to the Government's action, which they had made up their minds to oppose in future—by force if necessary. Notwithstanding this serious outlook of the labour problem I am still hopeful of getting the numbers required by next April. I sent down another special runner a week ago to Mr. Johnson for labour, and hope that results will be satisfactory."

The same question is referred to in the President's Inaugural Address in January, 1916, issued by the Government Printing Office.

Extracts from the Inaugural Address of President D. E. Howard, dated January 3rd, 1916

" A most flattering development has been observable in the work of the Bureau of Internal Revenue, a branch of the Treasury service hitherto much neglected by the Government and looked upon with no little hostility by the people. This was undoubtedly due to the fact that the revenue controlled by this Bureau resulted from direct taxation, an income method always unpopular and which rarely works without friction in any government.

" Under the judicious direction of the Commissioner, however, the functions of the Bureau have been enforced with decreasing opposition and evasion, while the results obtained have shown a steady and encouraging progression. . . ."

" The large amount of cash reported for the last fiscal year was due to the substantial payments on account of Hut Tax made by the Chiefs and people of the Hinterland of Montserrado County, the collection of which was made by the Interior Department as an agency for the Bureau of Internal Revenue.

" The whole activity of the Bureau has been such as to engender much faith in its future service to

THE LIBERTY OF THE SUBJECT

the Government, provided the laws governing the same continue to be prosecuted as they have been, which it is our purpose to see is unremittingly done.

" Our sources of internal revenue have barely been touched, but as a step in the right direction has been made, we are determined that there shall be no retrogression."

When the then President's view of the methods used in the collection of Hut Tax is read side by side with that of the Chiefs, comment is superfluous, and it stands as a masterpiece of euphemistic suppression of the truth. The whole address is worth reading, with its bombastic use of " We and Our " suggestive of a crowned head, and its strictures on the Great Powers of the world then at war, ending with the belief in God because: " We still believe that, behind the dim unknown standeth God within the shadow keeping watch above his own." . . . " Notwithstanding the present disturbed state of the world, *We* are still in friendly relations with all foreign powers," has quite the Kaiser's touch.

Again in the message to the Legislature of 15th December, 1915.

Collection of Hut Tax

"The internal revenue in the form of taxes which has been received from these sections of the Interior may be taken as a true index of what would be the tangible benefits following the maintenance of a policy of equity, a policy for which we are honestly striving, but which is difficult to enforce owing to the fact that some Commissioners will persistently misinterpret and abuse their pro-consular functions. The new method adopted by the Government for the collection of taxes through the Chiefs and Kings will obviate much of the misunderstandings and complaints hitherto arising out of a system that was not well defined nor easy of accommodation."

Hypocrisy could scarcely be carried further than in these glossed statements of the occurrences detailed above, while the reference to the Commissioners and their doings continues the subversion of facts. It is well known in the country that these delegates of the Government devote their energies chiefly to feathering their own nests at the cost of the tribes, sending their plunder down to friends on the coast for sale.

THE LIBERTY OF THE SUBJECT

In the same message the following passage occurs:

" With an earnest desire to readjust the policy of the Government regarding certain native districts, as well as with a view to simplifying the many difficulties with which we have been therewith confronted, it has been found necessary and expedient to recall all Interior and coast Commissioners."

The new departure in collecting the Hut Tax would certainly necessitate this step unless each Commissioner had a sufficient escort to defend his life.

Part IV—Voluntary Contributions

And yet these inland native tribes are as lovable and as easily guided by kindness and Justice as those of other parts of the Interior of the west coast. As an example of their goodwill towards Government the following instance may be given. At the commencement of the European war Liberia was practically cut off from regular steamship communication with the outer world for some months. German ships were driven off the seas, and other " Lines " called only spasmodically, so that food became very scarce in Monrovia and other ports on the Liberian coast. The inland tribes, however, depending upon their own resources, had ample supplies of food, and were asked to send down rice, manioc, and other native foods, for the populations of the coast towns. The inland Chiefs responded nobly and generously, and on one of the main arteries from the Interior streams of carriers passed down loaded with food.

A competent observer reckoned that over 2,000 carriers passed through his property in the course of a fortnight, coming from the "High Bush," as the more distant part of the Interior is termed.

A few days afterwards some of them were on their way back, stating that their treatment in Monrovia by the President had been of the most ungrateful nature.

It should be here premised that, by native custom, the bearers of presents from Chief to Chief are always treated generously, as representing the donor, and are usually well fed and given a small present for their own gratification. Although they swarmed round the State House asking for food after their long trek none was given them, so that they had to beg food in many cases from those they had come to succour, while many of them were housed and fed by some of their own tribes in a settlement across the Mesurado River. They were sent back without rations for the journey, hurried out of the town, and had to beg food from towns on their road, or steal and eat raw manioc from plantations by the wayside. It was in this manner that the writer's informant became aware of their ungrateful reception, and on asking many of them

"How much Dash" (Anglice, present) "Each man get," he was shown by some an empty Teplitz, or soda water bottle, while others had nothing.

On inquiry some time after, he learnt that the rice and other foods had been stored in Monrovia and issued to the officials in lieu of their overdue salaries, while the native population of Monrovia, on whose behalf the requisition was made, received little if any of the generous gifts of their countrymen.

This may be compared with the extract before given from a formal report on the method of collecting Hut Tax in kind, and dealing with the carriers thereof, and although the collection of a tax may be regarded as a proceeding more or less of a domestic nature within the State, not justifying intervention, the sale of the carriers to a foreign Power in the former case raises the matter to what should be regarded as of the highest international importance. Another instance of the high handed treatment of that sacred question "The Liberty of the Subject" occurred more recently when recruiting for the native regiments was in full swing in the neighbouring British Colony of Sierra Leone. Over one hundred Mendi Boys crossed the frontier to evade the pressure, and arrived at Monrovia looking for work.

THE LIBERTY OF THE SUBJECT

They were detained and shipped off to Fernando Po by the Government of Liberia, or by its agents (the German firm holding the contract for shipping the Kroo-boys) and head money was collected upon them. These were British subjects seeking refuge in a friendly State, and were dealt with by the Liberian Government as if they were their own subjects.

It is said that this matter was brought to the knowledge of the British Consul-General in Monrovia in time, but whether this was the case or not the " Boys " were shipped away, possibly before diplomatic action was possible.

" The Love of Liberty " which brought the American negroes to Africa has not worn well in later years, and has never been fully extended to the peoples under their control. The " Bush Niggers," as the Liberians term their fellow citizens of the Interior, still fight among themselves without interference on the part of Government, while the spoil of battle in prisoners, men, women or children, is still bartered among themselves, and even sold to the Liberians under the euphemism of " Boys."

Part V—Traffic in "Boys"

Travelling in the coffee-growing districts it is a common sight to see a couple of youths, almost naked, struggling under the burden of a stout Liberian, sometimes of the softer sex, in a hammock, and followed by two or three more youths or men laden with heavy bags of coffee, on their way to the town for shipment. Irrespective of age these are "Boys"; in English, purchased slaves.

With reference to this subject Sir Harry Johnston writes as follows:

"Amongst the aborigines, the farther one retreats from the settled coast belt the more evident is it that slavery is still a powerful institution. According to Mr. Gow, who travelled amongst the Kpwesi people on the Dukwia River in 1904, there is constant civil war between various Kpwesi tribes or communities, in the course of which prisoners are made. As it would be easy for these prisoners to run back to their homes, the desire of the captors

THE LIBERTY OF THE SUBJECT

is to dispose of them for large or small sums to Mandingo traders, or to hire them as apprentices to the Americo-Liberian settlers. At one time, no doubt, the Mandingo did a very good business in the Liberian Hinterland. They bought hundreds, possibly thousands, of slaves every year, and took them to the Mandingo Plateau, whence they were dispersed among the Hausa, Fula, and Hausa traders who frequented Samory's empire before it was conquered by the French. But there has been a marked decrease in the demand for slaves by these Mandingo merchants since the whole of the upper Niger Basin was occupied by the French Government. No doubt the simultaneous British occupation of Northern Sierra Leone equally reacts on this condition, since in all directions the market for slaves is being closed. There does, however, remain—it must be admitted—a great temptation to the Liberio-American planters, and one that it is difficult to stem. Undoubtedly the system of apprentices does not differ markedly from legalized slave buying.

"The Liberian planter, we will say, goes inland and is offered boy and girl, or adult slaves, by some native Chief. He pays perhaps from two to three pounds value in trade goods for each human being, and to satisfy his own conscience calls them apprentices.

"These people are then conveyed—usually very willingly on their part—to his own plantation or place of business, where they settle down as cultivators. . . ."

Sir Harry Johnston holds that the evil done is not without good results, as the practice serves to "people the coast regions and to increase the number of civilized negroes growing up under Liberian laws, and to give these unfortunate outcasts, at any rate, a life of tranquillity and safety; whereas if they remained as slaves in the Interior they would be liable to ill-treatment and death on small provocation." This is as it may be; but the writer's experience is decidedly against the suggested ill-treatment of slaves by their captors, partly because the African almost invariably shows a kindly disposition towards children; moreover, if the tribe or Chief desires to get a good price for their captive the captive must be well-fed. An example of this toleration is given in the same chapter: "The 'king' of Twidi, for example, in the Sikon country behind the Kroo

A "KING'S" DAUGHTER, MIDDLE ST. PAUL VALLEY.

coast, has a special town for his slaves, who live there under no restrictions, except that they may not leave the king's district or country without permission. These slaves are not only of Kpwesi origin, but in some cases are actually Mandingo who have been captured by the Chiefs of the Interior and sold as slaves, or more likely have been born in captivity of slave parents. Mr. Gow writes that these Sikon slaves are well treated; much better so than many free-born people. Should a free boy wish to marry a woman from amongst the slaves, he has simply to give her a leopard's tooth (which is a sign of freedom) and she is then a free woman and can go away with him." There is little of ill-treatment of captives by their original captors in practice; and from the unclothed and miserable appearance of some of the " Boys " the writer has seen in the Settlements, they would probably welcome a change to a country home where food is plentiful and continual work to acquire riches for their owners is as yet unknown.

Sir Harry Johnston strikes the true note in his concluding sentence to the chapter from which the above extracts are taken when he says: "What is wanted as a corrective to the slave trade is the construction of roads, and the creation of a legitimate commerce in the forest products of the country."

Any of my readers who have perused the chapter on " Communications " can judge for himself how far off that desired millennium is when a century of settlement and sixty of constitutional government have resulted in merely touching the coastal fringe of the great territory claimed by the Republic.

But whether under the guise of " Boys," " Apprentices," " redeemed," or " recruited labour " or any other euphemism used by the Liberians to throw dust in the eyes of the world, the fact remains that human creatures are bought and sold to-day, not only in the Interior, but in the settled districts of Liberia; a state of affairs which calls for immediate remedy by some Power strong enough peremptorily to forbid the evil in the coastal districts and gradually stamp it out in the Interior.

Part VI—Personal Experience

My own introduction into the system under which "Boys" are acquired in Liberia happened in my camp one day. A lady of large proportions visited me to sell rice, mats, sweet potatoes, and other native products, which were carried by four stalwart young men following behind in single file.

Having purchased, I entered into general conversation, and learned through my interpreter that she was the queen of a small town higher up the valley. (Kings and queens are as common as barn-door fowls in Liberia.) In my then innocence, I congratulated her on her four stalwart sons. A look of disdain crossed the royal features as she rapped out something which was interpreted, "Dem, dey not my Picking, dey my boys (slaves)." I said "Domestic Slaves?" a status well understood as belonging to the family circles, but the reply was, "No, dey bought by me; I pay ten dollars each."

Covering my surprise both at the disclosure and the price, I inquired where one could purchase some, and was answered that "plenty lib for High Bush," as a free translation of Her Majesty's reply. I afterwards found that my Headman's knowledge of the ways of his fellow men in the Interior confirmed the lady's story, for on paying him off later with considerably over five pounds as accumulated wages, the question was asked, "What are you going to do with all that money?" and the reply was that he was married to the sister of a king in Pwessi country, and had not been able to keep up the necessary retinue for such an exalted state, and therefore had bowed his proud neck to serve the white man. (As far as my personal experience had gone he served well.) Now he could return to his town in affluence, but first he would go up into the High Bush and buy two slaves, perhaps three, and then, as the present king was old and had no sons, he would be king and would be all right. A sinister promise for the future of his king; but as he served well he would probably rule well, and especially so in that he had experience of the strict ideas of Justice which prevailed in a white man's camp.

On my way down to the port I stopped a day or two at a farm. Having expressed my views on the question of the traffic in "Boys," my host agreed,

THE LIBERTY OF THE SUBJECT

but pointed out that owing to the difficulty in persuading Government to uphold genuine contracts entered into by labourers resident in the coast settlements, it was either " Boys " or ruin; that all the farm work on the coffee plantations, with the exception of an overseer here and there, was carried on by " Boys "; and that so-called freemen were useless except as gangers or highly paid house servants. Some of these favoured few even owned " Boys " on their own account, who did farm work on the land of their owner or another Liberian; and he gave me an instance of the work of a large coffee plantation which was carried on entirely by this class of labour, supplemented by the " Boys " of neighbours when the coffee required picking. In direct confirmation he called his Headman (steward and butler), and the following conversation ensued:

" How many Boys you get now, Bakari? " " Four, Sir." " What they do? " " Work for my farm." " Massa want one Boy, can you get one? " " Suppose Massa wait leetle bit, Boys come from Pwessi country." " How much you pay for Boy now? " " Ten dollar for High Bush, twenty dollar for Monrovia."

I was unable to wait, or otherwise I might

have brought a living confirmation to England of the traffic in children which exists in Liberia unchecked by the rulers of the State, not more than say fifty miles from their capital. Having recounted my experiences in a house where I awaited my steamer in Monrovia, the host laughed and remarked that it would be true in the main, with perhaps an exception or two, to say that there was hardly an official of the Government from the President downwards, who did not possess a " Boy " in his household, instead of paying servants as we do in our Colonies; and, moreover, that there were underlings who descended to deeper infamy and purchased girls who were hired out to houses where there were no other women as wife or servants, and in some instances where there were wives who tolerated the relations between their husbands and the " girl servants." The degradation of the ethics and principles of the motto of the State could hardly go farther in practice, and as these incidents and the information were totally unsought I leave it for those Powers whose duty it is to rectify such a state of affairs in the twentieth century; to apply the necessary remedies for this crying evil.

It will be seen from the foregoing that, with the

THE LIBERTY OF THE SUBJECT 141

exception of the extreme measures of shedding blood to enforce labour, the "Liberty of the Subject" under the rule of the Liberian Government is practically in the same state as under Leopold of evil memory in former days in the so-called Congo Free State, and that while all other Governments of civilized nations in West Africa have practically eradicated slavery in all its worst forms, it still flourishes in a small negro State, which only exists on sufferance because of its highly advertised purity of purpose towards the African races.

CHAPTER V

EDUCATION

ALL the world will agree that education is the bounden duty of the rulers of a civilized community, state, or nation; and especially so, of the rulers of a Republic, where all men are supposed to be equal, and therefore entitled to an equal share of intellectual training with which to compete in the race for that inequality of wealth or power that is the goal of mankind even in a Republic. From the ruler of the State downward in the scale of Pastors and masters to the comparatively humble position of a parish clerk, an appointment of some sort or other is the heart's desire in any Democracy; and among African races where the bottom of the ladder is slavery, that desire to climb is inherent; and the flame of desire to be placed in even a little brief authority over his fellow men burns more fiercely than in the white races which have other pursuits than politics to absorb their ambitious desires.

Education is the qualification for entry in the race toward " The Sin by which the angels fell "; and it is the right of every citizen of the Republic to have a share in the facilities for attaining to a knowledge of the " three R's," in return for the taxation imposed by the State. As far as Government provisions for this equality of treatment are concerned there are no facilities for the population of the Interior.

Both in the past and in the present age the Pastors and spiritual leaders of the people of the Republic have done their duty nobly to one and all who desire to be educated, and albeit that the desire for education is extremely difficult to inculcate in the primitive races of the world, owing to the fixed idea that reading and writing is " white man's " monopoly, they have sometimes succeeded where older States have failed in this direction, because teachers and learners are of the same colour and race. The writer views with whole-hearted approval, therefore, the continuous effort of Liberian Pastors, which has succeeded in making a lawyer and legislator out of the son of the Chief of a coastal tribe in one generation, instead of the usual three required by some other States and other systems of education. At present such cases may be few and far between, but in many conversations the writer has enjoyed with the late Dr. Blyden, and others, he has been impressed by the phenomenal receptiveness of more cultured ideas, by some of the sons of Africa drawn both from indigenous and imported sources. These examples tend to show both the fertility of the mental soil as well as the excellence of the system of cultivating the intelligence of African races, through the medium of another African race, already permeated with a century or more of comparatively advanced ideas.

In this direction it is manifest to the present writer that if the Republic of Liberia had been given a firmer Government during its tutelage by races that have learned to govern themselves with honour and probity for centuries past, it might certainly by now have formed a nucleus of the local African nations, around which the latter might have learnt to govern themselves by the only means now known to the civilized world—that is, the education of the people to think for themselves—and thus they might have evolved the forms of Government best suited to Africans.

But, although the early fathers and their successors

up to the present day have recognized the high value of a liberal education being placed within the reach of all, successive Governments in recent times appear to have lost sight of their responsibility, and to have left the duty of educating the people to a few mission schools, and other educationary bodies, supported by voluntary effort and donations from philanthropic societies in the United States and elsewhere.

There is, however, an " Education Department," the Secretary of which holds Cabinet rank, and that there is a glimmering of sense in this direction of the duty of the rulers is shown by the following extract from the Inaugural Address of President Howard in January, 1916.

" We feel that the importance of the payment of the special School Tax has not been fully grasped. As some of the counties have reported practically nothing from this source, we believe our statement is perfectly justified. This tax was not imposed without good reason. Our literacy is altogether too low in the interests of good government and the permanency of the State.

" The Treasury was measuring up to its full

EDUCATION 147

capacity for school purposes without emasculating other indispensable functions of the Government. In the circumstances it was felt that the people would respond to the efforts of the Government without feeling that the step taken was a burdensome imposition. If we are to judge by the fruits of this educational tax we are bound to conclude that there is too much lethargy on the part of the citizens as regards education." (Inaugural Address of President Howard, 3rd January, 1916.)

Better late than never, but it seems rather late in the history of the Republic for the State to take up this question, and the extract given tends to confirm the emphatic statement made by an enlightened Liberian and quoted later on.

The Education Tax is imposed upon all residents within certain areas, or others who may come into those areas, also upon native labourers (through their employers), who come down from the Interior under engagement for a year's service; but as these are without their women and children it is difficult to see what benefits they receive for their money, while, according to the statements in the Presidential address, it remains unpaid by those permanently resident within those areas, whose families can take advantage of the schools.

Professor Starr says of these schools in his chapter upon education: " In 1912, Dr. Payne had under his direction ninety-one public schools in different parts of the Republic.

" Most of these schools were housed in buildings totally unsuited to their purpose; they were small, badly built and unsupplied with even the barest equipment. There are no book stores in Liberia, and there is a notable lack of suitable books for children's use; there are few blackboards and those of poor quality; the desks, seats, and other furniture are conspicuous either for their absence or poor quality. Teachers are frequently badly prepared; they not infrequently neglect their duties; the number of days of teaching is uncertain as often the teachers will be occupied with other work than that to which they are supposed to devote their time and attention. Salaries are very low and badly paid."

Mr. Deputie, once Superintendent of Education, in his report of 1905, said: " Lend a hand by your official acts that will tend to ameliorate the condition of the teachers in the public schools that they may receive a just recompense of reward.

EDUCATION

Some of these teachers, after serving faithfully during the quarter, receive only ten shillings on their bills (Government paper money), while many others of them receive not a shilling."

Further on he says: "The public schools are, however, probably less numerous, and certainly reach fewer scholars than the various mission schools conducted by the different denominations. At the time that Mr. Barclay (E. Barclay) made his report he claimed but sixty-five public schools to ninety mission schools. While the public schools reached 1,782 scholars, the mission schools had an attendance of 3,270 children. These mission schools very largely reach a native population; it is true that some Liberians attend them, but the larger number in attendance is from native families; all the schools located in native towns are, probably, under mission guidance.

"In some respects these schools are distinctly superior to the public schools of the Republic. Their teachers, with higher salaries, devote themselves with more energy to their work; text-books are supplied and the equipment for school work is better; the buildings, too, both in construction, lighting, and adaptation to their work, are better."

Now at the head of the chapter above quoted is an extract from a speech by a former President which says: "For support given to education, Liberia holds the first place among West African administrations. Sierra Leone, with a revenue six times greater than Liberia, spends only one-fifth of the sum devoted by our State to the cause of public instruction."

Either the speaker is taking to the credit of the State all the work of the missions or the State expenditure does not reach the work for which it is ear-marked. Possibly it forms part of the reserve funds entitled " Hog," which is the synonym of the " Pork Barrel " of the United States.

On submitting this apparent conflict of evidence to a high authority on Liberian matters who has resided in the Republic for years, his remarks were: " The Government spends very little upon the education of the people excepting in the way of salaries for officials of the Department of Education. The whole credit for the education of the Liberian people may be ascribed to teachers and workers outside the Government circle."

These voluntary workers, supported by charitable associations, are often in conflict with the authori-

EDUCATION

ties (whose neglected duty they are fulfilling) on the score of fussy interference by officials.

Taking Sir Harry Johnston's figures (although in the absence of reliable statistics these can only be regarded as approximate) as to the numbers in the Interior, there are in round numbers 12,000 Liberio-Americans; 30,000 natives in touch with these who know a little English and something of civilization; and 2,000,000 of untouched natives. Professor Starr thinks the last is over-estimated, and it is true that since Sir Harry Johnston's book was published there may have been a decrease of territory which would reduce the number considerably, but if 1,000,000 only is taken, the natives are about eighty-five to one as compared with the Liberians. The former receive very little benefit or tuition at the hands of their rulers, and thus continue to constitute a menace to the cause of the civilization of West Africa.

CHAPTER VI

SANITATION

THE ethical foundations on which good municipal or domestic government are built are pure air, pure water, pure food, with honesty of purpose on the part of those placed in authority over us to ensure that these ideals are realized in such ways that they are within reach of the bulk of the people, subject to natural conditions beyond the control of man. It is therefore the manifest duty of the supreme government of a State to make such legislative and financial provisions as will enable the municipal or subordinate officials to carry on their duties in these matters both energetically and continuously.

These terms are axiomatic in the domestic government of civilized communities, and so important are these factors in the well-being of a State that the rulers may be classed as good, bad or indifferent, in such degrees as they are fulfilled, seeing that they materially affect not only the living, but also the future generations of subjects to be born to the State.

Judged by these standards the Government of Liberia is a ghastly failure, and the lack of even attempts at sanitary measures throughout the towns of the Republic is a standing menace to the residents, and, by infection or contagion, to the people of the Interior.

In Monrovia, the capital of the Republic, it may be said at once that none of these ideals of good government have received attention. The air which once was pure is now polluted by lack of cleanliness, together with the natural drainage and accumulation of the surface filth of the town, to the harbour on one side, and to the swamps on the other side of the promontory on which the greater part of the town stands. The water supply is drawn from wells sunk on the hillside, and supplied by percolation through fissures in the plutonic rocks by which the promontory and Cape of Mesurado are formed geologically.

There is no general source of supply other than that of wells sunk in the rock-formation on which the town is built, and the water is supplied by natural faults or rifts in the formation. In some cases there is a cesspool in the same small yard as the well, and all over the town it is only a question of comparative hydrostatic pressure whether the flow is from the well to the cesspool, or from the cesspool to the well. The water conserved in the rock formation depends upon the rain fall which is fortunately very heavy even for West Africa; but the dry season is well marked also, and it is at the end of the drought that the danger becomes a standing menace to the residents of Monrovia, especially Europeans; and, although care is taken by the latter to filter water for household use, and to drink only aerated waters, these measures are not effective against the germs of malignant malaria or typhoid fever.

There is no general filtration scheme for the native population; but as there are no reliable health statistics, it is not possible to compare the death rate with those of other communities. It may be remarked, however, that the native population is more or less immune to the above mentioned diseases, and this is also said to be the case with yellow fever.

In these conditions earth closets would appear to be imperative, but the cesspool system in all its pernicious forms prevails, where the more primitive seclusion of the " Bush " is not available.

With regard to the control of the quality of food which is consumed by the community, there is no examination by a properly constituted and capable authority of the meats and fish exposed for sale in the markets, and in the case of one enlightened Liberian neither of these were consumed in his house unless he or his wife bought direct from the butcher when the beast was killed, or from the fishing boat on its arrival, owing to the danger of food being poisoned by infected flies and other causes. There is no analysis of other classes of food imported into the country.

It may be advanced that the population of a West African town will eat what it likes in spite of authority; but in other communities samples are analysed before food can be offered for sale in the stores or public markets.

There are sporadic attempts at street cleaning by prisoners, and some years ago an energetic Mayor of Monrovia undertook a crusade against the accumulated filth of the back yards of the citizens, which was subsequently piled in heaps in the middle of the streets and there left to rot and breed a plague

SANITATION

of flies that would have made a respectable show against the Egyptian one of ancient script. As the Government love and dislike swings like a pendulum between the admirers of its productive territories, and the German influence was then predominant, the site generally chosen for these demonstrations of sanitary activity was in front of the house, office, or bank of a British resident. To those who have experience of the filth of an African dust-heap these conditions are well known, and for those who have not they are better left to the imagination.

It may be remarked by some that if the community likes to live in an unsanitary state they only injure themselves, and that the state of affairs described rebounds on the Liberian alone, but that is not the true view. In a measure, England, France, and America are sponsors for the good government of the African tribes under the Republic of Liberia; and although they, with other Powers, signally failed in their duty in the case of the Congo Free State, that was more due to international jealousies than to lack of goodwill; while now the friction has disappeared and the three powers can intervene in Liberia without fear of any serious consequences. So long as they trade with the Black

Republic, and their merchants live there, it is "up to them" to secure the same sanitary security for the lives as they would for the liberty of their subjects. A parallel case would be that of a householder in London or the suburbs whose back yard was in a filthy state, and who argued that it was his yard and he would not spend money on keeping it clean. The neighbours who suffered from his neglect would not agree with his views, and would move the authorities to interfere, so that the upholder of filth would emerge from the contention a cleaner and wiser, if poorer, man.

While our steamers, for the purpose of commerce and communications with our traders, have to transport passengers and goods to and from other Colonies, the sanitary state of the port of Monrovia is a menace to the general health of the West African coast, and to the ports of European nations trading thereto.

There are in Monrovia no hospitals or professional nurses; there is no Government Dispensary; at times there are no doctors, therefore there is no proper diagnosis, or official report to the Government by a professional man of infectious or contagious diseases, which in other ports would

SANITATION

suggest quarantine; and without these precautions the port is a danger to the whole coast.

It is probable that all these matters have been duly reported by successive British Consul-Generals from time to time, but they have no control of dust-heaps or cesspools in a foreign town, and unless such reports are read in the light of exposing evils which require eradication, and maintain that it is the duty of the British Government to take steps to protect their subjects and other Colonies from infectious diseases consequent upon the neglect of the Government of Liberia, there is very little chance of the above stated ideals of good government being realized in Liberia, or of its progress in sanitary matters becoming rapid enough to assimilate with the happier African communities under the flags and protection of England and France.

CHAPTER VII

COMMUNICATIONS

It has been laid down ever since the days of the Roman Empire, and probably before, that roads and other facilities for travel and transport are essential to good government, also to the control and protection of the governed. In the County of Montserrado, outside a radius of twenty-five miles from Monrovia, roads are practically non-existent, and the only instance of what may be classed as a "road" was made at the cost of the Government, but by English engineers, to facilitate the operations of a company. They laid a tramway on it, and even this one road has fallen into disrepair. In former days paths from the Interior to the coast were kept clean by mutual consent, as they are in other parts of Africa; and those from village to village, by each village clearing to the common boundary. What were known as "Customs" were charged to travellers on their merchandise and for safe conduct; and the system, established from time immemorial, worked well.

The Liberian Government, seeking revenue, now taxes the Chiefs and native tribes within their reach, who thus feel dubious of the advantages of keeping up the roads which lead tax-gatherers to their villages; and main paths, which a few years ago were kept brushed and open, are now overgrown with weeds and bush.

"Customs" or "Dashes" for safe conduct are still in vogue among inland tribes, although in some districts known to the writer the track is hardly wide enough to walk upon safely, even without the incumbrance of a pack on the back or head. The individual Liberian takes kindly to this form of collecting personal revenue, and the writer has met heavily laden women and children on their way to Monrovia making a detour by overgrown bush paths round the village ruled by a Liberian, to avoid the "Customs" imposed when passing through.

An instance is also recorded of an attempt to charge one shilling per head on some newly recruited "Boys" from Bassa County, who were travelling with the agent of their employer to his farm, on the score that they were strangers in Montserrado

County and therefore must pay a poll tax for crossing the land of a Liberian planter, although they were on the so-called main road.

Personal Instance

Passing through a village, my hammock and carriers were stopped by the Headman for " Customs." I was ahead, walking for a change, and was called back by my interpreter, who ran after me, saying, " Palaver lib for town."

The claim was seriously made by a snuff and butter coloured individual, and compounded eventually for one shilling. The claim was made out to be based on his being a free Liberian with a town (Anglice " Farm ") through which the road ran, and which he claimed to have kept in repair.

Of bridges in the Interior there are none worthy of the name excepting those built by the English company referred to above, on the road they made for Government; all others in the valley of the St. Paul's River, which the writer has crossed or heard of, may be best described by the name used in Africa of " Monkey Bridges." [1] The term may be regarded

---

[1] In the Hinterland of Liberia, where the influence of the coastal Government is as yet very slight, there are many suspension bridges over the larger rivers, most ingeniously con-

as a humorous reference to the danger of crossing unless one still retains the sense of balance and the agility of our far-away ancestors.

Professor Starr, in dealing with this subject, writes: "'Problems' closely associated with the matter of production is the question of transportation. It is one of the most serious that faces Liberia.

"If produce cannot be taken to the coast it is of no value in the development of trade. There are practically no roads in Liberia to-day. As in the Dark Continent generally, narrow foot trails go from town to town; to travel over them is always in single file; the path is but a few inches wide and has been sharply worn into the soil to a depth of several inches by the passage of many human feet. As long as transportation is entirely by human carriers such trails are serviceable, provided they are kept open. A neglected trail, however, is soon overgrown and becomes extremely difficult to pass; that a trail should be good it is necessary that the brushwood and other growth should be cut out at fairly frequent intervals. Often, however, the Chief of a given

structed by local "kings." One across the Upper Lofa River, in existence two or three years ago, was 290 feet across from support to support.

A LIBERIAN "ROAD" NEAR THE COAST.

village does not care to remain in communication with his neighbours, and intentionally permits the trail to fall into disuse. There is a feeling, too, surviving from old customs, that trails are only passable with the permission and consent of the Chiefs of the towns through which they run; Chiefs have always exercised the right of closing trails whenever it pleased them; they have expected present ('dashes') for the privilege of passing. If now large trade is to be developed in the matter of native produce, it is absolutely necessary that the trails be kept in good condition and that free passage over them be granted to all. Much of the energy of the Government must of necessity be directed toward these ends. At the best, however, there is a limit to the distance over which produce can be profitably transported on human backs; there must be a very large inherent value in such produce to warrant it being carried more than a three days' journey by human carriers. It is not only the labour involved in transportation, but the loss of time that renders this problem important. The richest resources lie at a great distance in the Interior; even with good trails it is impossible to utilize them . . ." And again: " Improved trails and roads are of the highest importance to the Republic for several reasons:

"(*a*) For intercourse: only by means of them can ready and constant intercourse be developed between the different elements of the population; no great development in trade, no significant advance can be made without constant intercourse; it must be easy for the Government to reach and deal with the remotest natives of the far Interior; it is equally important that peoples of the neighbouring towns have more frequent and intimate contact with each other; it is necessary that the members of different tribes come to know other tribes by daily contact.

"(*b*) For transportation: there is no reason why even the existing trails should not be covered with caravans carrying produce to the coast.

"(*c*) For protection: at present the movement of the Frontier Force from place to place is a matter of the highest difficulty; if trouble on the frontier necessitates the sending of an armed force, weeks must elapse before the enterprise can be accomplished; until the present unsatisfactory conditions of trails can be done away with, Liberia is in no position to protect her frontiers."

The desiderata enumerated above are truisms and

are also axioms of settled government derived from the earliest stages of civilization; yet after many years of so-called government, observers of the present decade still find the Interior with its communications in the old primitive state, and these fundamental questions neglected.

CHAPTER VIII

EXTERNAL RELATIONS

Part I—Political Difficulties

BEFORE describing in detail the failure of Liberian rulers to keep step with their neighbours in the civilization of inland tribes it should be premised that the President's Writs are practically ineffectual outside a twenty-five mile radius from Monrovia, and less from other ports on the coast. There is no adequate force or means of enforcing obedience.[1] It follows that outside the radius mentioned the Government attitude must be persuasive towards the tribes, and that they rule by sufferance on the part of their subjects rather than by power.

Although more or less powerless, Liberian rulers are intensely jealous of their neighbours. It is the

---

[1] The Republic maintains a black force, armed with modern weapons, called the " Liberian Frontier Force." It is officered partly by American negroes, and is used in their wars with the aboriginal native tribes. It is also used as an armed civil police force.

inability to enforce Justice in the Interior of the State, and on its boundaries with other nations, that has led to continual bickering with England and France, with pleas to the United States for protection from their neighbours.

If a recalcitrant Chief, in either British or French territory, has defied his District Commissioner or Commandant, as the case may be, and is therefore "wanted," he has only to skip across the Liberian boundary, and from that position of comparative security, "cock snooks" at his baffled pursuers.

Trespass upon the territories of Sovereign States by the properly constituted armed forces of another State is a *casus belli* by International Law, and the regular course under these conditions is to apply for extradition or expulsion. In the case of a criminal, however, all civilized States are bound to deny asylum and, moreover, to aid in the capture and extradition.

In either of these cases appeal to Monrovia has been found to be futile; and even if the wish to play the game of a just and powerful State were present in the spirit, the body corporate is weak, and there is no sufficient physical power or control available. This results in *non possumus* after much delay,

EXTERNAL RELATIONS 171

and permission has occasionally been given to the neighbouring Power to arrest the culprit on Liberian territory, which, of course, means occupation by an armed force of British or French, more or less long drawn out according to circumstances. Then follow complaints from the Liberian Government to other Powers that their territory is being occupied by the Power in question and taken from them. This is more or less true as events have shown; but if the Republic cannot carry out what International Law calls " effectual occupation " and simply depends on mythical explorations of long ago for her title, since when no effort has been made either to bring the boundary tribes into subjection by the establishment of posts, or by Missionary effort,[1] it stands to reason that the Great Powers, who have taken in hand the civilization of the whole of the African Continent, cannot stand aside and allow a black spot to remain on the map outside the circle of International Law, with no roads, railways, telegraphs, or any of the outward and visible signs which constitute the enlightenment of Africa and help on its progress toward a

---

[1] Since this was written the Liberian Government has established a number of military posts in the Interior, garrisoned by the " Liberian Frontier Force."

stage of civilization suited to its people: a progress which is now making such giant strides in other parts of the west coast. Since 1894, when the writer first visited West Africa, he has witnessed the great regeneration of the whole of that part of the continent —with the exception of Liberia. She alone has stagnated, and is even now with less hope of making a successful African State than ever, despite the benevolent toleration she has enjoyed owing to the sentimental protection extended to her even during the eighties of last century, when the " Scramble for Africa " was in full swing.

Part II—Other Opinions

To give a hearing to the other side of the question the reader is referred to Professor Starr's work, " Liberia," where among the problems which remain to be solved he will find the history of the " Boundary Questions " from 1848 to recent dates. On the whole, the question is dealt with historically, that is, in an impartial spirit, with perhaps a slight bias in favour of the little State. This may be gathered from his introductory paragraph, quoted below; but as these vexed questions and their history are recorded in the chancelleries of the two Powers in question, to which apparently Professor Starr has not referred, one can only regard his conclusions as drawn from one side of the question at issue.

He says: " The most pressing and ever urgent question which the Republic has to face is the protection of its frontiers against aggression; Liberia has two powerful neighbours, both of which are land hungry and are continually pressing upon her borders; she has already lost large slices of her territory and is still menaced with further loss." This is the keynote of the chapter on "Boundary Questions," and one is hardly inclined to quarrel with a champion who thinks it his duty to uphold the interests of a small and weak State against two powerful neighbours; for both of the nations in question have poured out untold blood and treasure to support those identical principles. The historian in question has painted his picture as to aggression and land hunger, from the Liberio-American point of view, while the reason for the continually recurring boundary squabbles is as stated above, that the territories in question have never been effectively occupied or controlled, although tacitly allowed to be within the Liberian sphere of influence, always provided, as the lawyers say, that the proper measures were taken to bring them into line. This claim to lands or territory, many miles away from the seat of Government, and out of reach of the arm of Liberian law, could have been made good during all these years, and there would have been an end to the squabbles. It is manifestly

EXTERNAL RELATIONS 175

impossible for England and France to tolerate an African " Alsatia " or " No Man's Land " on the boundaries of their own carefully governed States. " Hence these tears."

Sir Harry Johnston also gives a history of the " Frontier Questions," and remarks in this connection: " President Barclay's arguments against the French assumption that the absence of Americo-Liberian settlements in the far Interior argues a lack of Liberian occupation are that he considers all the negroes inhabiting Liberia to be Liberians, and has not the slightest desire to displace native born negroes by Colonists born on the coast. This is a perfectly sound doctrine; but of course the present weakness of the civilized Americo-Liberian Government on the coast is that it has no sure means of maintaining law and order between tribe and tribe, and between all these tribes in the Hinterland with regard to their relations with the French and English possessions across the frontiers. The British have borne with patience the occasional lawlessness of Kissi, Kondo, and other tribes on the Sierra Leone boundary, together with the gun running, namely, the passing of guns and ammunition in defiance of Customs regulations from Liberia into the recently agitated Hinterland of Sierra Leone.

"France complains of similar lawlessness on the north-east and north-west frontiers of Liberia. On the other hand the Liberian Government retorts that the Mahommedan negroes who are now French subjects are eating steadily into the Liberian Hinterland. They are penetrating into the north-east parts of Liberia, firstly as peaceful traders, and secondly as somewhat exclusive Colonists. They cut down the forest and take possession of the country little by little, driving back the forest-dwelling people towards the heart of Liberia.

"President Barclay's assumption that all the negroes inhabiting the somewhat fluctuating territory claimed as Liberia are Liberians, may be consoling as a reason for the lack of Government control by the establishment of outposts in the Interior, but it is non-effective in the practical sense, and the title of 'Liberian' which is used by the natives generally to designate the Liberio-American (when 'American' is not used in the same sense) would be regarded as more or less an insult by the members of the large inland tribes who are as proud of their own country and tribal names Vai, Kroo, Grebo, etc., as we are of the name of England and Englishman.

"There is a touch of humour in the peaceful penetration of the Hinterland by the Vai people, the finest nation in North-West Africa—warriors, merchants, travellers, at one time part of the great Kingdom of Melli, which was the first negro State to accept Mahommedanism, in the ninth century, rebelling against and conquering its suzerain power, the Empire of Jenne in 1329, and practically ruling the Fouta Jallon, with the head waters of the Niger, Senegal, Gambia, and all the great rivers with their upper valleys round to the St. Paul's and Cavalla.

"Until broken by Ischia the Great, and made subject to the newly arisen Empire of Timbuctoo in the sixteenth century, the Malinkes (Mellinkes?), as the French call them, or Mandingoes, of which the Vai is held to be of the most ancient stock, were, and are still, the Colonizers of North-West Africa; although since the advent of the white man they can no longer make raids with the Koran in one hand and the Scimitar in the other; so that, having learnt the lesson of 'Peaceful Penetration,' they now practise it upon the powerless Liberian State."

Part III—Personal Conclusions

The Great Powers have no use for a second "Haiti," or San Domingo on the Continent of Africa, however pure its aspirations may be in theory, unless they can be translated into better efforts for the good of those over whom the Republican Government has been placed in authority.

As to the Government of the Republic of Liberia it will be gathered from the text that there is little hope of reform.

From the President downwards, they are a set of *poseurs*, with high-sounding titles, but lacking the manners and courtesy generally associated with the higher stations of life in other countries, and with little regard for their word or their engagements.[1] They will make an appointment to meet a man to discuss the most serious matters of business, or questions pertinent to their departments, and keep

[1] These words were written during the Presidency of Mr. Howard.

EXTERNAL RELATIONS 179

him waiting their pleasure exactly in the manner of an African Chief who desires in that way to impress both the visitor and his own tribe with the fact that he is a " Big Man." Even after having waited for the interview, the visitor to the State Departments of Liberia will be at times informed by a messenger that the official in question will be unable to see him. Emperors, Kings, Presidents, and rulers of the world's great States keep their engagements with both their subjects and foreigners, but the President of Liberia is above these conventions, and, with one or two exceptions, his officers of State follow the lead faithfully. Further than that, the spirit of pomposity runs through the entire warp and woof of their civic life. Every man from the top downwards tries to impress his " bigness " on the man a little lower down. This inherent desire in mankind, derived from our arboreal ancestors and their relative positions on the family tree, is curbed amongst civilized peoples by the substitution of the theory and practice of *noblesse oblige*, but the little African Republic has not yet learned its lessons in either courtesy or diplomacy.

At the celebration of the National Anniversary, 16th July, 1915, the Honourable J. J. Dossen, the

Chief Justice, was the chosen orator; but the celebration was held without the orator as he did not appear at the function, or in the procession. The absence of the " Lead " arose out of a " palaver " with the Governor of the Province in which the celebration was held on the question of the order of precedence *ex officio*, the orator claiming as Chief Justice to rank " with and after," as we say, the Vice-President of the Republic. The Governor went one better and claimed to represent the President himself in the county. The order subsequently given under the hand of the President in the above quoted issue of the *Gazette* lays it down that: at public functions where neither the President nor the Vice-President is present, the Chief Justice must be accorded first place. Truly a pitiful example of petty pride, but one which characterizes the official class, or what is locally known as " The Long Coats," from their love for the conventional frock coat and silk hat of many obsolete forms which they wear on every possible occasion.

These criticisms may be regarded by some as beside the main question at issue, namely that of the ability of the Liberio-American to govern properly the African races under his control, and, moreover, coming from a professed lover of the African races generally to savour of ill-nature; but those who have worked on the West African coast will admit that the picture is not overdrawn, and that the same desire to ape the big white man and his ways is general amongst educated negroes, even where under control of white heads of departments. It is only because that control is lacking in Liberia that the official class is more arrogant than in our Colonies. This leads to the ethical point, exemplified in other black negro Republics, that the negro races may be easily governed by an autocracy, which is really a hierarchy in his primitive state, for the African Chief is seldom a despot; but that in the present state of racial evolution, a republican form of government spells failure.

A faint hope there was that the negro race after a century of evolution under American civilization might form an exception to the sweeping statement; but the individual negro has not learnt the lessons of that great school for men of all nations, nor the self-abnegation which makes the highest in the State the servant of the people.

The ethical question, as to how much longer this failure of the fundamental ideas of proper government is to be tolerated at the expense of the indigenous tribes of Liberia, is one which should receive the immediate attention of the Powers that have shouldered the "white man's burden" in the noble work of the regeneration of Africa.

CHAPTER IX

DEVIL WORSHIP

Part I—Original Ideals

THE path of duty on which the founders of the Liberian State set out was that of a mission to their African brethren, whom they fervently desired to convert from their worship of Jujus, idols and other heathen creeds, to Christianity. To that noble ideal they sacrificed health, and even their lives, in trying to inculcate the only doctrines around which civilization will flourish; suffering from hunger, want, disease, and the lack of remedies; struggling against the opposition of those for whom they had sacrificed all that made life easy in their home country, and even fighting with earthly weapons to maintain their foothold on the margin of the Great Dark Continent, without material support either from their own or other nations.

All honour to them. Their names are inscribed

in letters of gold on the scroll of African history with those martyrs who have died for others and the pure ideals of Christianity.

Their successors pursued the same straight path with varying success so long as the simple form of patriarchial or hierarchial rule lasted: then came ambition, with the clouding of the ideals, extension of boundaries and erection into an independent Sovereign State, with the natural corollary of joining in the "Scramble for Africa," after the example set to them by older and more powerful States. With the Republic founded on the lines of the United States of America, the little State also acquired a President, Senate, and the usual Officers of State, the election to which positions of power and emolument, although nominally in the hands of the people, was confined to the original stock of Liberian-Americans and their descendants, and remains so to this day with a few exceptions.

The original ideals were upheld by successive missions from time to time, and some of the children of the indigenous races within a restricted area around the capital and the chief towns on the coast are educated and brought up in the Christian religion; but the inland tribes, as far as change of

DEVIL WORSHIP 185

creed is concerned, still remain in the same benighted condition in which the founders of the settlement found them a century ago.

The old ideals, however, have gradually faded amongst the political ambitions of the Republic; and although a pale reflection of the past rulers, priest, prophet, and martyr, is still evident in the prayers at the opening of the Legislature or Courts, and in the addresses of the President of the day to the people, the power has passed into the hands of the professional politician, chiefly, as in other States, the lawyer-politician. The Church has been relegated to the background, with revenues dependant upon voluntary subscriptions and subsidies from America, and is now almost powerless to extend its efforts for good to the tribes of the Interior for lack of support from the State. So that, while church bells are ringing daily and several times a day in Monrovia and other centres on the coast, calling the faithful to prayer as of old, the further activities of the successors of the founders in that direction are chiefly those of educating children within the same restricted areas; and any attempt at conversion of the bulk of the tribes to Christianity has ceased.

It thus follows that both State and Church being powerless in the Interior, "Devil worship," as it is locally called, is rampant.

Nearly every town in the Interior possesses a "Devil Bush" and a "Devil Doctor," and the latter, among intensely superstitious races, makes much pecuniary profit, and has much influence over the actual Chief and the people of the district.

Part II—Present Conditions

As an example of this power for evil the experience of the manager of an English company which held mining rights over part of the Republic may be given.

Wishing to prospect an adjoining valley to that in which the works were situated, he sent a messenger to the Headman of the village in that valley to hire a house as depot and quarters for the prospectors. In the ordinary course the villagers would have welcomed the advent of the company's men, as the establishment of works there would carry in its train both work and wealth to the people, some of whom had been working at the previous headquarters for years past. The reply came back, "No white man can come to the town, Big Devilman lib there."

As the company was quite within its legal rights in prospecting, an appeal was made to the Head Chief farther up country, who sent his second-in-command down to the manager to hear the "palaver," but in spite of a " good dash " (Anglice, generous present) he said, " This Devil palaver, big palaver," adding that it must be taken to the big Chief, again farther up country.

After some more delay, a message came down that the " palaver " must await the coming of the Big Chief to settle it. After some further delay the manager threatened to invoke the authority of the Government, which only elicited the contemptuous remark, " Governor (the natives adopt the English title for the ruler of the State) no fit to come into High Bush," and there, perforce, the matter rested, as even if a white man went there to assert the rights of the company, he would certainly run grave danger of being poisoned at the instigation of the Devil Priest, while even the " Boys " belonging to the town refused to work until the " palaver " was settled. The location was within thirty miles of the capital, and this is in a State which complains that it cannot attract European capital in order to open up the undoubted mineral wealth of the Interior.

The question will naturally arise : " Why not appeal to Government to maintain the company's right of entry to the valley? "

The answer to that is that Government is powerless to guard one against poison in the daily food or water when one's own servants are under the malign influence of the Devil Doctor; and there are not wanting examples of the danger of so doing in the past history of the country, so that the best way is to keep out of the range of the Devil Doctor's machinations, unless he is "squared," which, of course, was the origin of the "palaver"; but to submit to this blackmail would mean endless trouble and expense in the future.

His activities deal with the tribal customs as well as with the occult. In this direction he is credited with miracles, such as killing boys and making them alive again in the depths of the Devil Bush, on payment of a fee of course, with the undertaking of making them invulnerable to death in the future. He deals with trials of accused persons by poison (by administration of what is called "Sassandra" or "Sass Water"), circumcision of youths and maidens, makes barren women fruitful, or procures abortion, according to desire.

It will be recognized, therefore, that the Devil Doctor is a power in the land to be reckoned with; and when it is added that the emoluments or fees are exorbitant and yet are freely paid, owing to the superstitious fears of the people, or their belief in his power for good or evil fortune, the difficulty of dealing with his cult all over the Interior is manifest.

As an example of the Devil Doctor's machinations the following story was told by a resident:

His Headman asked for twenty-five dollars, partly in advance, as his pay was only ten dollars a month. His master naturally asked him what he wanted such a large sum for. " My woman want to go for Devil Bush get medicine for make pickin." " How much money she take?" "One sheep, one white fowl, one case gin, ten dollars."

It is almost unnecessary to add that the advance was not made, much to the satisfaction of the " Boy," who took his master's point of view as to the probable course of treatment his wife would undergo, but had been worried by the woman and the Devil Doctor to agree to paying, if his master would lend the money.

Two of the writer's own men assured him that they had been initiated into the mysteries of the Devil Bush: that they had been killed (by drinking poison) and brought to life again by the Devil

MUD WALLS ROUND A VILLAGE, FRANCO-LIBERIAN BORDER.

DEVIL WORSHIP

Doctor, when they were young boys: that no evil chance could now befall them, because their parents had paid the Devil Doctor to protect them, and now they themselves gave him " dash."

When one reflects that this state of affairs exists within twenty-five miles of Monrovia and extends throughout the pagan races of the Interior after nearly a century of occupation by the Liberian-American Missions and the Republic, the question arises whether it is not the duty of the European sponsors to give the native races a better form of Government and more effective rulers.

The whole of the evil business of Witch Doctors, Devil Doctors, Jujumen, and the murderous associations of Leopards, Crocodiles, Snakes, and other secret societies have been firmly repressed by the Governments of other States, who found the same conditions thirty years ago in some of the new Protectorates; and it follows that it is the duty of those Powers to bring pressure on the Liberian Government to also put their house in order, or to do it for them, in the interests of the native races of the Interior.

Of course the white man is never able to penetrate

the arcana of these mysteries, owing to the impassable gulf that ever lies between the white and black races with regard to ethnical secrets, and all experience shows that it is unwise for an individual to attempt it: but with a strong Government it is different, as the action is more or less impersonal, and the evil powers in question hardly know where to strike; moreover, firm action on the part of the authorities is sure to gain a multitude of adherents to their cause from the mass of the population, who scarcely believe in the Mumbo-Jumbo business, but are afraid to initiate any resistance to its power as they would be marked down and would pay for it with their lives after being tortured with devilish ingenuity for days.

It is owing to this all-pervading fear that many Liberio-Americans have " Gone Fanti," as they say on the coast when any educated man relapses towards primitive customs and habits; while there is good authority for suspecting that many of the higher officials are in the grip of native secret societies, and that some of their devilish rites are practised in Monrovia itself periodically.

It follows that the people of Liberia may look in vain to their present rulers in the hope of relief from this incubus on their well-being which now permeates their daily life, and forms a most formidable obstacle to any real advance on the path of progress which leads to a higher state of civilization.

CHAPTER X

THE SUMMING UP

Part I—Recapitulation

THE sum of the charges made herein does not constitute the whole case against the rulers of the Liberian Republic.

Others could be formulated of toleration, of immoral and vicious criminal practices on the part of some of the community, which are punished by imprisonment and ostracision in better governed communities, but which, in Liberia, are glossed over or ignored; even in the case of some who have been entrusted with high judicial office or the education of the young.

The natural consequence of such acts being allowed to pass unpunished is transmission to the rising generation, and their perpetuation in the community.

These charges, however, are apart from those of misrule and oppression of their native subjects, and there are not wanting, amongst the ruling classes, many just men who decry this evil state of blindness to immorality on the part of the Government, but who are powerless to correct it under the present conditions.

The indictment that has been laid against the present rulers of Liberia, therefore, may be summed up as follows:

1. Breach of the Constitution under which the State received the recognition and protection of other civilized Powers.

   (*a*) Maladministration of Justice and corruption in high places.

   (*b*) Toleration of a system of slavery.

   (*c*) Infraction of the liberty of the subject for the purpose of making pecuniary profit by deportation of their native subjects.

2. Toleration of, and implication in, secret native societies, the aim of which is the intimidation of those who offend any members thereof.

3. Lack of ordinary measures for the protection of public health, to the danger of their own subjects

THE SUMMING UP

and those of other nations residing in, or trading to, Liberia.

4. Failure in conciliating the native tribes, leading to incessant civil and intertribal wars.

General oppression by force of arms by officers of the Government in the collection of taxes and imposed fines amongst the native tribes without judicial inquiry.

These alone form a formidable list for any so-called civilized Government to answer, and, as a matter of course, they imply an extension of misrule on the part of those to whom authority is delegated, right down the line of officialdom.

The main charges can be sustained by reputable witnesses, but for obvious reasons no names are given, nor should they be required to bear public witness if they desire to reside or have interests in Liberia; but the main facts stated become common knowledge with those who have resided in the country for a few months and have gained the confidence of the better part of the community, and of the natives.

Part II—The Judgment

Having appeared as counsel for the natives of Liberia, and summed up the case against the Liberio-American rulers, following the precedent of Lewis Carrol's " Snark," the author now proceeds to deliver judgment. Lest it should be deduced from the foregoing statements that he is an advocate of the extinction of the Liberian Republic and the annexation of its territories to England or France, he desires to associate himself with all the other authorities quoted in this work, and to speak as a candid but friendly critic, whose sincere sympathy is with the effort of those Liberians who really desire to learn to rule themselves, and to extend their rule to the indigenous tribes now nominally under their control.

Sir Harry Johnston's plea for more time to settle these problems—" It is surely not too much to ask from the kindliness and civilization of Europe that the poor little Americo-Liberian Republic shall have

THE SUMMING UP 199

grace accorded to it—say another fifty years—within which to show how it can bring into an orderly condition the not very large territory entrusted to its charge"—expresses the tolerant sympathy of all friends of the African races towards the Liberian-American experiment.

But the author has shown, and has supported by extracts from other friends and observers, that during the past no real progress has been made in properly governing the inland tribes, and that the present tendency is retrogressive; so that unless radical changes are made it would be asking too much of the indigenous tribes, that they should have to bear the burden of the experiment during a further apprenticeship of the Liberio-Americans to the science of governing a State composed of heterogeneous peoples so sharply divided from each other by hereditary traits, religion, and native customs; while their rulers are so far apart from them in the same attributes as to be regarded as aliens by the natives of their own Continent of origin. Moreover, the art of self-government as a free community is laboriously acquired through many generations, and by many stages, often by bitter experiences, and is not born in a more or less primitive race.

The more advanced nations of the world that have allowed the "poor little Americo-Liberian Republic" to struggle on for so many years, without imposing a term of tutelage upon the inexperienced rulers thereof, as guardians of the infant State and in the interests of the indigenous peoples of the territory left under their control, are responsible to-day for the decadence of the Republic and the lack of progress in the Interior.

We ourselves, in the past, have laid it down in official documents that we are only the trustees and guardians of the African races under our own control; and, before the keen competition of other powers for possessions in Africa, our governors were instructed that we were only in that country to preserve peace and to teach the Africans to govern themselves. We have stood by and looked on while a community of Africans, only one generation removed from slavery, have been trying to evolve good government for themselves out of a book, the A.B.C. of which they had never learned, with a cut-and-dried Constitution that they could not understand. They had just emerged from a primitive state of being, coupled with servitude, where independent thought was unnecessary; while the

THE SUMMING UP

instinct of orderly and just administration only becomes ethnically apparent in the human race after many generations of liberty of thought and action. So that with all our kindly acts of protection and assistance which have been consistently evidenced to the Liberian Republic, owing partly to past jealousy of other Powers, we have been guilty of sins of omission toward the tribes of the Interior in not demanding that the rulers should receive Residents or Commissioners from us or other Powers who would extend the happy conditions of our own Protectorates to Liberia. The Powers interested have been careful to introduce receivers where the collection of moneys on their behalf is concerned; and the collection of the interest and sinking fund on the loan as a first charge on the revenue is not altogether unconnected with the desperate measures adopted by the Government of Liberia to obtain an internal revenue without those necessary preliminaries of opening up the Interior to trade and commerce which would fill the coffers of the State automatically. With us human lives and liberties weigh more than money, and we shall be fulfilling a higher duty if we introduce proper control to ensure those privileges to the natives of Liberia.

Formerly, owing to international jealousies, this could not have been done without the danger of being charged with that " Land Hunger," mentioned by Professor Starr; but now the Great War is over a new era should dawn in West Africa; and in the new conditions which should prevail there will doubtless occur an opportunity for Great Britain to take the lead, as the oldest friend and protector of the African races, in coming to the assistance of the little negro State, and so arranging matters with the other Powers as to have a free hand in the regeneration of Liberia.

There is a clear and insistent call upon all the nations which have worked hand in hand for years past toward the betterment of Africa and its peoples, and have so recently been embroiled in war for the rights and liberties of smaller and weaker States, to intervene between the present Government of Liberia and its indigenous African subjects, and either conjointly, or by the delegation to one Power, to take up the duty of opening up her Hinterland, bring the tribal Chiefs under proper control, and allow the undoubted wealth of her territories in natural products, both mineral and vegetable, to flow into her national coffers: or, by insisting upon the appointment of European officials to carry out such radical changes and reforms as will ensure recognition of the right of the native races to just and upright treatment at the hands of their rulers. Above all to safeguard in the future the inherent right of the native races to the enjoyment of Liberty and Freedom under the Republic which claims sovereignty over their lands, property, and lives, in harmony with the laws of civilized nations, in common with native races under the control of our own Colonies and of other Powers engaged in the preservation, betterment, and civilization of the negro races on the Continent of Africa.

INDEX

African League, The, 67, 68
African Mail, The, 75, 77
Alphabet, Negro, 61
American Colonization Society, 33
Apprentices, 133, 136

BALLARD, MAJOR, 55
Banei, 55
Barclay, President E., 149, 175, 176
Barra, 53, 54
Bassa County, 68, 162
Bathurst, 54
Belli Tribe, 121
Blama, 121
Blood feuds, 50, 73
Blyden, Dr., 145
Boundary questions, 173-177
British Government, 53, 78, 96, 103, 109, 133, 170, 175
Browne, Captain, 55
Buildings, 40, 41, 63, 64
Bureau of Internal Revenue, 124
" Bush niggers," 58, 69, 131

CALDWELL, 73
Caste feeling, 58
Cavalla, 177
" Ceded Mile," 53
Character of Liberians, 71, 72
Chester (Cruiser), 77
Children, African attitude towards, 52, 134
Christianity in Liberia, 183-185
Churches, 41, 185
Circuit Court, 94
Civil war in Liberia, 55, 56, 131, 197
Clay Ashland, 73

Colleges, 41, 64
Congo Free State, 141, 157
Consolidated Loan, 35
Constitution, Liberian, 33, 105, 106, 196
Costume, native, 60, 61
Crozierville, 73
" Customs," 161, 162, 163
Customs Department, 35

" DASH " (COMMISSION), 113, 130, 162, 188
Debt, imprisonment for, 86
Decadence of Liberia, 62, 63, 64
Delafosse, 59, 64, 65, 67
Deputie, Mr., 148
" Devil Bush," 186, 190
" Devil Doctor," influence of, 186-191
Dossen, Honble. J. J., 179

EDUCATION DEPARTMENT, 146-150
Education, native views on, 144
Education, support given to, 150, 151
Ellis, G. W., 66
Exploitation, foreign, 70, 71
Extradition difficulties, 170, 171

FEES OF COURT, 84, 85, 89, 90, 91
Fernando Po, 122, 131
Food supply, 156
Fouta Jallon, 177
French Government, 54, 133, 170, 175, 176
French Ivory Coast, 45
Fula, 133

INDEX

Gambia, 53, 54, 177
Gangawoo, 121
German Colony, 38, 113, 114
Germanic sympathies, 76, 78, 79
Ghendimah, 61
Glassi, 55
Government, 41, 42, 55, 56, 72, 79, 140, 145, 146, 150, 154, 160, 162, 165, 166, 169, 172, 174, 175, 176, 178-182, 189, 191-203
Government Gazette, appeal in, 73, 74, 75
Gow, Mr., 132
Grebo, 176
Greenleaf, 33

Haiti, 178
Hausa, 133
Hawkins, Captain, 55
" Hog," 39, 150
Hospitals, lack of, 158
Howard, President, 51, 55, 56, 75, 78, 178
Hut Tax, 124-127, 130

Ischia the Great, 177

Jenne, 177
Johnston, Sir Harry, 36, 61, 71, 132, 134, 135, 151, 175, 198
Judges, conduct of Liberian, 101, 102
Judges, salaries of, 103
Judiciary system, 92-99, 106, 107
Judiciary system, attempts at reform, 100-102
Jujumen, 191
Justice, Liberian conceptions of, 82 *et seq.*
Justices of the Peace, 83, 84, 85, 92, 93

King, Secretary, 78
Kissi, 175
Kondo, 175
Kpwesi, 132
Kroo, 58, 60, 73, 74, 75, 77, 118, 119, 120, 176
Kroo-boys, hiring of, 118, 119, 120
Kroo rebellion, 77, 78

Lamin, Case of, 86, 87, 88
Land, sale of, 48, 49
Land, tenancy of, 46, 47, 51
Laws, Liberian, 34
Lawyers, 70, 81, 95, 96, 97, 98, 100
Liberians (Liberio-Americans), 34, 42, 44, 46, 56, 57, 59, 60, 62, 64, 65, 69, 70, 71, 72, 79, 93, 109, 110, 131, 133, 137, 149, 150, 151, 163, 169-172, 175, 176
Liberian Colleges, 41, 64, 97
Liberian Frontier Force, 77, 122, 166, 169, 171
Liberian Order of Redemption, 44
Litigation, African fondness for, 85, 98
Lofa River, Upper, 164

Mahommedan negroes, 176, 177
Mandingo, 60, 133, 135, 177
Manienka, 61
Manual labour, attitude towards, 69
Martin, Lieut., 55
Melli, 177
Mendi, 130
Mesurado, 45, 48, 129, 154
Miller, Lieut., 55
Mission of 1822, 45-51, 109, 110, 183, 184
Mission schools and colleges, 41, 145, 149, 150
Mission stations, 41, 191
Momolu Massaquoi, 61
" Monkey Bridges," 163
Monrovia, 39, 40, 41, 44, 59, 64, 68, 73, 79, 81, 121, 122, 123, 129, 130, 131, 139, 140, 154, 155, 161, 163, 169, 170, 185, 191
Monthly Court, 94
Montserrado County, 124, 161
Mulba, King, 121, 122

Native Chiefs, 45, 46, 47, 48, 49, 50, 89, 90, 111, 112, 113, 114, 121, 122, 123, 133, 162, 188
Native customs, 45, 46, 47, 49, 129, 183-193

INDEX

Native subjects, traffic in, 121, 122, 123, 132-141, 196
Natives shipped to Fernando Po, 122, 131
Native tribes, character of, 128
Natural resources, 71
Niger, 177
"Nucleus of Liberians of the Ancient Time," 65, 67

PAHN (CAPE PALMAS), 55
"Palavers," 49, 50, 85, 88, 89, 188
Parliamentary elections, 66, 67, 68
Parliamentary franchise, 68
Pawning of individuals, 114, 115, 116
Payne, Dr., 148
"Peaceful Penetration," 46, 176, 177
Perseverance Island, 45, 48
Peter, King, 48, 49
Planh, 55
Political " Bosses," 95, 96
Political corruption, 68, 69, 70, 103, 104, 105, 196
Political difficulties, 169-172
Portuguese West Africa, 113
President, Inaugural Address of, 1916, 55, 123, 124, 125, 146, 147
President, Liberian, 34, 35, 72, 76, 106, 107, 129, 140, 141, 169, 178-182
Probate Court, 94
Public health, 154-159, 196

REPRESENTATIVES HALL, 63
Republic, establishment of Liberian, 47, 109, 110
Republican Party, 66
River Cess, 55
Roads, 161
Rock Cess, 55

ST. MARY, ISLAND OF, 54
St. Paul River, 73, 123, 163, 177
Sanitary conditions, 39, 40, 154-159
School Tax, 146, 147
Secomb, 55

Secret Societies, 191, 196
Senegal, 177
Senegambia, slave bought in, 112, 113
Sierra Leone, 45, 53, 120, 130, 133, 150, 175, 176
Sikon slaves, 134, 135
Sinoe, 55, 77
Slavery, "domestic," 114, 115
Slavery, extirpation of, in Africa, 111
Slavery in Liberia, prohibited in 1847, 109, 110
Slaves, 109 et seq.
Starr, Professor Frederick, 45, 48, 52, 57, 58, 59, 64, 65, 66, 67, 72, 148, 151, 164, 173, 202
State Officials, 35, 36, 37, 38, 70, 93, 126, 143, 178-182, 197
Status of natives, 57, 58, 59, 93, 121, 122, 123, 151
Supreme Court, 96, 106

TAPPI, 55
Taxation, 39, 122, 124-127, 146, 162, 197
Teachers, 148, 149
Tenancy of land, 46, 47
"Three bars," 54
Transportation, problem of, 164-167
Travelling in Liberia, 56, 161-168
Treasury, Liberian, 35, 38, 39, 79, 85, 103, 104, 146
Twidi, King of, 134, 135

UNITED STATES, 33, 34, 37, 42, 55, 77, 78, 80, 92, 109, 170

VAI, 58, 60, 61, 176, 177
Virginia, 73, 74

WARFARE, AFRICAN, 51
Water supply, 154, 155
Whig Party, 66, 68
White Plains, 73
Wireless stations, 41
Witch Doctors, 87, 88, 191

Printed for Messrs. H. F. & G. Witherby by
The Northumberland Press Ltd., Newcastle-on-Tyne